JAMESTOWN EDUCATION

Timed Readings Plus
in Mathematics

BOOK 5

**15 Two-Part Lessons with Questions for
Building Reading Fluency and Comprehension**

D1552128

Mc Graw Hill **Glencoe**

New York, New York   Columbus, Ohio   Chicago, Illinois   Peoria, Illinois   Woodland Hills, California

JAMESTOWN EDUCATION

Glencoe

The McGraw-Hill Companies

ISBN: 0-07-872663-8

Send all queries to:
Glencoe/McGraw-Hill
8787 Orion Place
Columbus, OH 43240-4027

2 3 4 5 6 7 8 9 10 021 10 09 08 07 06

CONTENTS

To the Student

    Reading Faster and Better   2

    Mastering Reading Comprehension   3

    Working Through a Lesson   7

    Plotting Your Progress   8

To the Teacher

    About the Series   9

    Timed Reading and Comprehension   10

    Speed Versus Comprehension   10

    Getting Started   10

    Timing the Reading   11

    Teaching a Lesson   11

    Monitoring Progress   12

    Diagnosis and Evaluation   12

Lessons   13–72

Answer Key   74–75

Graphs   76–78

TO THE STUDENT

You probably talk at an average rate of about 150 words a minute. If you are a reader of average ability, you read at a rate of about 250 words a minute. So your reading speed is nearly twice as fast as your speaking or listening speed. This example shows that reading is one of the fastest ways to get information.

The purpose of this book is to help you increase your reading rate and understand what you read. The 15 lessons in this book will also give you practice in reading mathematics-related articles and in preparing for tests in which you must read and understand nonfiction passages within a certain time limit.

Reading Faster and Better

Following are some strategies that you can use to read the articles in each lesson.

Previewing

Previewing before you read is a very important step. This helps you to get an idea of what a selection is about and to recall any previous knowledge you have about the subject. Here are the steps to follow when previewing.

Read the title. Titles are designed not only to announce the subject but also to make the reader think. Ask yourself questions such as What can I learn from the title? What thoughts does it bring to mind?

What do I already know about this subject?

Read the first sentence. If it is short, read the first two sentences. The opening sentence is the writer's opportunity to get your attention. Some writers announce what they hope to tell you in the selection. Some writers state their purpose for writing; others just try to get your attention.

Read the last sentence. If it is short, read the final two sentences. The closing sentence is the writer's last chance to get ideas across to you. Some writers repeat the main idea once more. Some writers draw a conclusion—this is what they have been leading up to. Other writers summarize their thoughts; they tie all the facts together.

Skim the entire selection. Glance through the selection quickly to see what other information you can pick up. Look for anything that will help you read fluently and with understanding. Are there names, dates, or numbers? If so, you may have to read more slowly.

Reading for Meaning

Here are some ways to make sure you are making sense of what you read.

Build your concentration. You cannot understand what you read if you are not concentrating. When you discover that your thoughts are straying, correct the situation right away. Avoid distractions and distracting situations. Keep in mind the information you learned from previewing. This will help focus your attention on the selection.

Read in thought groups. Try to see meaningful combinations of words—phrases, clauses, or sentences. If you look at only one word at a time (called word-by-word reading), both your comprehension and your reading speed suffer.

Ask yourself questions. To sustain the pace you have set for yourself and to maintain a high level of concentration and comprehension, ask yourself questions such as What does this mean? or How can I use this information? as you read.

Finding the Main Ideas

The paragraph is the basic unit of meaning. If you can quickly discover and understand the main idea of each paragraph, you will build your comprehension of the selection.

Find the topic sentence. The topic sentence, which contains the main idea, often is the first sentence of a paragraph. It is followed by sentences that support, develop, or explain the main idea. Sometimes a topic sentence comes at the end of a paragraph. When it does, the supporting details come first, building the base for the topic sentence. Some paragraphs do not have a topic sentence; all of the sentences combine to create a meaningful idea.

Understand paragraph structure. Every well-written paragraph has a purpose. The purpose may be to inform, define, explain, or illustrate. The purpose should always relate to the main idea and expand on it. As you read each paragraph, see how the body of the paragraph tells you more about the main idea.

Relate ideas as you read. As you read the selection, notice how the writer puts together ideas. As you discover the relationship between the ideas, the main ideas come through quickly and clearly.

Mastering Reading Comprehension

Reading fast is not useful if you don't remember or understand what you read. The two exercises in Part A provide a check on how well you have understood the article.

Recalling Facts

These multiple-choice questions provide a quick check to see how well you recall important information from the article. As you learn to apply the reading strategies described earlier, you should be able to answer these questions more successfully.

Understanding Ideas

These questions require you to think about the main ideas in the article. Some main ideas are stated in the article; others are not. To answer some of the questions, you need to draw conclusions about what you read.

The five exercises in Part B require multiple answers. These exercises provide practice in applying comprehension and critical thinking skills that you can use in all your reading.

Recognizing Words in Context

Always check to see whether the words around an unfamiliar word—its context—can give you a clue to the word's meaning. A word generally appears in a context related to its meaning.

Suppose, for example, that you are unsure of the meaning of the word *expired* in the following passage:

> Vera wanted to check out a book, but her library card had expired. She had to borrow my card, because she didn't have time to renew hers.

You could begin to figure out the meaning of *expired* by asking yourself a question such as, What could have happened to Vera's library card that would make her need to borrow someone else's card? You might realize that if Vera had to renew her card, its usefulness must have come to an end or run out. This would lead you to conclude that the word *expired* must mean "to come to an end" or "to run out." You would be right. The context suggested the meaning.

Context can also affect the meaning of a word you already know. The word *key,* for instance, has many meanings. There are musical keys, door keys, and keys to solving a mystery. The context in which the word *key* occurs will tell you which meaning is correct.

Sometimes a word is explained by the words that immediately follow it. The subject of a sentence and your knowledge about that subject might also help you determine the meaning of an unknown word. Try to decide the meaning of the word *revive* in the following sentence:

> Sunshine and water will revive those drooping plants.

The compound subject is *sunshine* and *water*. You know that plants need light and water to survive and that drooping plants are not healthy. You can figure out that *revive* means "to bring back to health."

Distinguishing Fact from Opinion

Every day you are called upon to sort out fact and opinion. Because much of what you read and hear contains both facts and opinions, you need to be able to tell the two apart.

Facts are statements that can be proved. The proof must be objective and verifiable. You must be able to check for yourself to confirm a fact.

Look at the following facts. Notice that they can be checked for accuracy and confirmed. Suggested sources for verification appear in parentheses.

- Abraham Lincoln was the 16th president of the United States. (Consult biographies, social studies books, encyclopedias, and similar sources.)

- Earth revolves around the Sun. (Research in encyclopedias or astronomy books; ask knowledgeable people.)

- Dogs walk on four legs. (See for yourself.)

Opinions are statements that cannot be proved. There is no objective evidence you can consult to check the truthfulness of an opinion. Unlike facts, opinions express personal beliefs or judgments. Opinions reveal how someone feels about a subject, not the facts about that subject. You might agree or disagree with someone's opinion, but you cannot prove it right or wrong.

Look at the following opinions. The reasons these statements are classified as opinions appear in parentheses.

- Abraham Lincoln was born to be a president. (You cannot prove this by referring to birth records. There is no evidence to support this belief.)

- Earth is the only planet in our solar system where intelligent life exists. (There is no proof of this. It may be proved true some day, but for now it is just an educated guess—not a fact.)

- The dog is a human's best friend. (This is not a fact; your best friend might not be a dog.)

As you read, be aware that facts and opinions are often mixed together. Both are useful to you as a reader. But to evaluate what you read and to read intelligently, you need to know the difference between the two.

Keeping Events in Order

Sequence, or chronological order, is the order of events in a story or an article or the order of steps in a process. Paying attention to the sequence of events or steps will help you follow what is happening, predict what might happen next, and make sense of a passage.

To make the sequence as clear as possible, writers often use signal words to help the reader get a more exact idea of when things happen. Following is a list of frequently used signal words and phrases:

until	first
next	then
before	after
finally	later
when	while
during	now
at the end	by the time
as soon as	in the beginning

Signal words and phrases are also useful when a writer chooses to relate details or events out of sequence. You need to pay careful attention to determine the correct chronological order.

Making Correct Inferences

Much of what you read *suggests* more than it *says*. Writers often do not state ideas directly in a text. They can't. Think of the time and space it would take to state every idea. And think of how boring that would be! Instead, writers leave it to you, the reader, to fill in the information they leave out—to make inferences. You do this by combining clues in the story or article with knowledge from your own experience.

You make many inferences every day. Suppose, for example, that you are visiting a friend's house for the first time. You see a bag of kitty litter. You infer (make an inference) that the family has a cat. Another day you overhear a conversation. You catch the names of two actors and the words *scene, dialogue,* and *directing.* You infer that the people are discussing a movie or play.

In these situations and others like them, you infer unstated information from what you observe or read. Readers must make inferences in order to understand text.

Be careful about the inferences you make. One set of facts may suggest several inferences. Some of these inferences could be faulty. A correct inference must be supported by evidence.

Remember that bag of kitty litter that caused you to infer that your friend has a cat? That could be a faulty inference. Perhaps your friend's family uses the kitty litter on their icy sidewalks to create traction. To be sure your inference is correct, you need more evidence.

Understanding Main Ideas

The main idea is the most important idea in a paragraph or passage—the idea that provides purpose and direction. The rest of the selection explains, develops, or supports the main idea. Without a main idea, there would be only a collection of unconnected thoughts.

In the following paragraph, the main idea is printed in italics. As you read, observe how the other sentences develop or explain the main idea.

Typhoon Chris hit with full fury today on the central coast of Japan. Heavy rain from the storm flooded the area. High waves carried many homes into the sea. People now fear that the heavy rains will cause mudslides in the central part of the country. The number of people killed by the storm may climb past the 200 mark by Saturday.

In this paragraph, the main idea statement appears first. It is followed by sentences that explain, support, or give details. Sometimes the main idea appears at the end of a paragraph. Writers often put the main idea at the end of a paragraph when their purpose is to persuade or convince. Readers may be more open to a new idea if the reasons for it are presented first.

As you read the following paragraph, think about the overall impact of the supporting ideas. Their purpose is to persuade the reader that the main idea in the last sentence should be accepted.

Last week there was a head-on collision at Huntington and Canton streets. Just a month ago a pedestrian was struck there. Fortunately, she was only slightly injured. In the past year, there have been more accidents there than at any other corner in the city. In fact, nearly 10 percent of all accidents in the city occur at the corner. This intersection is very dangerous, and a traffic signal should be installed there before a life is lost.

The details in the paragraph progress from least important to most important. They achieve their full effect in the main idea statement at the end.

In many cases, the main idea is not expressed in a single sentence. The reader is called upon to interpret all of the ideas expressed in the paragraph and to decide upon a main idea. Read the following paragraph.

> The American author Jack London was once a pupil at the Cole Grammar School in Oakland, California. Each morning the class sang a song. When the teacher noticed that Jack wouldn't sing, she sent him to the principal. He returned to class with a note. The note said that Jack could be excused from singing with the class if he would write an essay every morning.

In this paragraph, the reader has to interpret the individual ideas and to decide on a main idea. This main idea seems reasonable: Jack London's career as a writer began with a punishment in grammar school.

Understanding the concept of the main idea and knowing how to find it is important. Transferring that understanding to your reading and study is also important.

Working Through a Lesson

Part A

1. **Preview the article.** Locate the timed selection in Part A of the lesson that you are going to read. Wait for your teacher's signal to preview. You will have 20 seconds for previewing. Follow the previewing steps described on page 2.

2. **Read the article.** When your teacher gives you the signal, begin reading. Read carefully so that you will be able to answer questions about what you have read. When you finish reading, look at the board and note your reading time. Write this time at the bottom of the page on the line labeled Reading Time.

3. **Complete the exercises.** Answer the 10 questions that follow the article. There are 5 fact questions and 5 idea questions. Choose the best answer to each question and put an X in that box.

4. **Correct your work.** Use the Answer Key at the back of the book to check your answers. Circle any wrong answer and put an X in the box you should have marked. Record the number of correct answers on the appropriate line at the end of the lesson.

Part B

1. **Preview and read the passage.** Use the same techniques you

used to read Part A. Think about what you are reading.

2. **Complete the exercises.** Instructions are given for answering each category of question. There are 15 responses for you to record.

3. **Correct your work.** Use the Answer Key at the back of the book. Circle any wrong answer and write the correct letter or number next to it. Record the number of correct answers on the appropriate line at the end of the lesson.

Plotting Your Progress

1. **Find your reading rate.** Turn to the Reading Rate graph on page 76. Put an X at the point where the vertical line that represents the lesson intersects your reading time, shown along the left-hand side. The right-hand side of the graph will reveal your words-per-minute reading speed.

2. **Find your comprehension score.** Add your scores for Part A and Part B to determine your total number of correct answers. Turn to the Comprehension Score graph on page 77. Put an X at the point where the vertical line that represents your lesson intersects your total correct answers, shown along the left-hand side. The right-hand side of the graph will show the percentage of questions you answered correctly.

3. **Complete the Comprehension Skills Profile.** Turn to page 78. Record your incorrect answers for the Part B exercises. The five Part B skills are listed along the bottom. There are five columns of boxes, one column for each question. For every incorrect answer, put an X in a box for that skill.

To get the most benefit from these lessons, you need to take charge of your own progress in improving your reading speed and comprehension. Studying these graphs will help you to see whether your reading rate is increasing and to determine what skills you need to work on. Your teacher will also review the graphs to check your progress.

About the Series

Timed Readings Plus in Mathematics includes five books at reading levels 4–8, with one book at each level. Book One contains material at a fourth-grade reading level; Book Two at a fifth-grade level, and so on. The readability level is determined by the New Dale-Chall Readability Formula and is not to be confused with grade or age level of the student. The books are designed for use with students at middle school level and above.

The purposes of the series are as follows:

- to provide systematic, structured reading practice that helps students improve their reading rate and comprehension skills

- to give students practice in reading and understanding informational articles in the content area of mathematics

- to give students experience in reading various text types—informational, expository, narrative, and prescriptive

- to prepare students for taking standardized tests that include timed reading passages in various content areas

- to provide materials with a wide range of reading levels so that students can continue to practice and improve their reading rate and comprehension skills

Because the books are designed for use with students at designated reading levels rather than in a particular grade, the mathematics topics in this series are not correlated to any grade-level curriculum. Most standardized tests require students to read and comprehend mathematics passages. This series provides an opportunity for students to become familiar with the particular requirements of reading mathematics. For example, the vocabulary in a mathematics article is important. Students need to know certain words in order to understand the concepts and the information.

Each book in the series contains 15 two-part lessons. Part A focuses on improving reading rate. This section of the lesson consists of a 400-word timed informational article on a mathematics topic followed by two multiple-choice exercises. Recalling Facts includes five fact questions; Understanding Ideas includes five critical thinking questions.

Part B concentrates on building mastery in critical areas of comprehension. This section consists of a nontimed passage—the "plus" passage—followed by five exercises that address five major comprehension skills. The passage varies in length; its subject matter relates to the content of the timed selection.

Timed Reading and Comprehension

Timed reading is the best-known method of improving reading speed. There is no point in someone's reading at an accelerated speed if the person does not understand what she or he is reading. Nothing is more important than comprehension in reading. The main purpose of reading is to gain knowledge and insight, to understand the information that the writer and the text are communicating.

Few students will be able to read a passage once and answer all of the questions correctly. A score of 70 or 80 percent correct is normal. If the student gets 90 or 100 percent correct, he or she is either reading too slowly or the material is at too low a reading level. A comprehension or critical thinking score of less than 70 percent indicates a need for improvement.

One method of improving comprehension and critical thinking skills is for the student to go back and study each incorrect answer. First, the student should reread the question carefully. It is surprising how many students get the wrong answer simply because they have not read the question carefully. Then the student should look back in the passage to find the place where the question is answered, reread that part of the passage, and think about how to arrive at the correct answer. It is important to be able to recognize a correct answer when it is embedded in the text. Teacher guidance or class discussion will help the student find an answer.

Speed Versus Comprehension

It is not unusual for comprehension scores to decline as reading rate increases during the early weeks of timed readings. If this happens, students should attempt to level off their speed—but not lower it—and concentrate more on comprehension. Usually, if students maintain the higher speed and concentrate on comprehension, scores will gradually improve and within a week or two be back up to normal levels of 70 to 80 percent.

It is important to achieve a proper balance between speed and comprehension. An inefficient reader typically reads everything at one speed, usually slowly. Some poor readers, however, read rapidly but without satisfactory comprehension. The practice that this series provides enables students to increase their reading speed while maintaining normal levels of comprehension.

Getting Started

As a rule, the passages in a book designed to improve reading speed should be relatively easy. The student should not have much difficulty with the vocabulary or the subject matter. Don't worry about the passages being too easy; students should see how quickly and efficiently they can read a passage.

Begin by assigning students to a level. A student should start with a book that is one level below his or her current reading level. If a student's reading level is not known, a suitable starting point would be one or two levels below the student's present grade in school.

Introduce students to the contents and format of the book they are using. Examine the book to see how it is organized. Talk about the parts of each lesson. Discuss the purpose of timed reading and the use of the progress graphs at the back of the book.

Timing the Reading

One suggestion for timing the reading is to have all students begin reading the selection at the same time. After one minute, write on the board the time that has elapsed and begin updating it at 10-second intervals (1:00, 1:10, 1:20, etc.). Another option is to have individual students time themselves with a stopwatch.

Teaching a Lesson

Part A

1. Give students the signal to begin previewing the lesson. Allow 20 seconds, and then discuss special terms or vocabulary that students found.

2. Use one of the methods previously described to time students as they read the passage. (Include the

20-second preview time as part of the first minute.) Tell students to write down the last time shown on the board or the stopwatch when they finish reading. Have them record the time in the designated space after the passage.

3. Next, have students complete the exercises in Part A. Work with them to check their answers, using the Answer Key that begins on page 74. Have them circle incorrect answers, mark the correct answers, and then record the number of correct answers for Part A on the appropriate line at the end of the lesson. Correct responses to eight or more questions indicate satisfactory comprehension and recall.

Part B

1. Have students read the Part B passage and complete the exercises that follow it. Directions are provided with each exercise. Correct responses require deliberation and discrimination.

2. Work with students to check their answers. Then discuss the answers with them and have them record the number of correct answers for Part B at the end of the lesson.

Have students study the correct answers to the questions they answered incorrectly. It is important that they understand why a particular answer is correct or incorrect. Have them reread relevant parts of a passage to clarify an answer. An effective cooperative activity is to have students work in pairs to discuss their answers, explain why they chose the answers they did, and try to resolve differences.

Monitoring Progress

Have students find their total correct answers for the lesson and record their reading time and scores on the graphs on pages 76 and 77. Then have them complete the Comprehension Skills Profile on page 78. For each incorrect response to a question in Part B, students should mark an X in the box above each question type.

The legend on the Reading Rate graph automatically converts reading times to words-per-minute rates. The Comprehension Score graph automatically converts the raw scores to percentages.

These graphs provide a visual record of a student's progress. This record gives the student and you an opportunity to evaluate the student's progress and to determine the types of exercises and skills he or she needs to concentrate on.

Diagnosis and Evaluation

The following are typical reading rates.

Slow Reader—150 Words Per Minute

Average Reader—250 Words Per Minute

Fast Reader—350 Words Per Minute

A student who consistently reads at an average or above-average rate (with satisfactory comprehension) is ready to advance to the next book in the series.

A column of X's in the Comprehension Skills Profile indicates a specific comprehension weakness. Using the profile, you can assess trends in student performance and suggest remedial work if necessary.

Demographics and City Planning

Most of Manhattan in New York City is laid out on a grid, with streets running at right angles to each other. The principles of geometry are the basis of such a plan. Created by city officials in 1807, the plan included 12 north-and-south avenues, each 100 feet in width, and cross streets ranging from 60 to 100 feet in width. Manhattan has a total area of 33.8 square miles—23 of land and 10.8 of water. The city planners designed Manhattan according to what seemed best for the number of people living there, given the amount of land. They could not have known about the traffic conditions and crowding that would result a century later. They had no way of knowing that more than 1.5 million people would one day pack themselves into an area planned for 400,000. City planners now know that the early city officials would have used Manhattan's existing space better if they had doubled the number of north-and-south avenues and created half the number of cross streets.

Today's city and town planners try to predict how fast an area will change and by how much. They try to make accurate plans for growth based on demographics. Demography is the study of human population. Demographics are descriptions of the characteristics of a population, often presented in statistical terms. When compared over several years, demographic data provide information on changes and trends in a population's characteristics. People who study the demographics gather information about the population such as age range, gender, income, family size, and education level. The statistics may present totals, such as the number of people living in a 10-square-mile area. Or they may present an average number of people per household or the average number of children under 10 per household.

By studying the demographics of an area, city planners can design communities that will serve existing and future populations. For example, in June 2004, the York Region in Ontario, Canada, had a population of 873,000. This was an increase of more than 261,500 people since 1996. Since 2001 the York population has been growing by about 38,000 people a year. Any change in the number of people living in an area will have an effect on services, such as buses and the water supply, and on economics and the environment. York's planners will study the demographics of the region to plan development and services for its growing population.

Reading Time _____

Recalling Facts

1. The Manhattan city planners
   - ❑ a. designed the grid according to what seemed best for the number of people living there.
   - ❑ b. decided how long it would take to build a community.
   - ❑ c. calculated the future needs of the population.

2. Demographics are descriptions of the _____ of a population.
   - ❑ a. characteristics
   - ❑ b. statistics
   - ❑ c. planning

3. In demographics, the characteristics of a population are presented
   - ❑ a. as totals.
   - ❑ b. in statistical terms.
   - ❑ c. as plans.

4. Manhattan was originally planned for
   - ❑ a. 38,000 people.
   - ❑ b. 1.5 million people.
   - ❑ c. 400,000 people.

5. Age, sex, and income are characteristics of
   - ❑ a. a population.
   - ❑ b. demographics.
   - ❑ c. a statistic.

Understanding Ideas

6. Area planners learn about changes in the characteristics of a population by
   - ❑ a. studying trends and changes in the area's demographics over a number of years.
   - ❑ b. studying the planning mistakes of other areas.
   - ❑ c. looking at details of city planning.

7. What does proper planning *not* offer a community?
   - ❑ a. a better use of space for existing and future populations
   - ❑ b. better city services
   - ❑ c. population growth

8. You can conclude from reading the passage that an area's demographics may include statistics on
   - ❑ a. the number and kinds of trees.
   - ❑ b. how many families own pets.
   - ❑ c. the number of families expected to leave in 10 years.

9. Demographic data that city planners would be likely to study would include
   - ❑ a. number of family members who live at home.
   - ❑ b. number of friends who visit per day.
   - ❑ c. family members' favorite colors.

10. Which of the following statements is *not* true?
    - ❑ a. The characteristics of a population include past and future statistics.
    - ❑ b. Statistics provide a mathematical summary of an area's population.
    - ❑ c. Demographics provide a summary of an area's population.

14

Who Uses Demographics?

Demography is one way to study population. It can be a useful tool for understanding the world we live in. Demographics are the characteristics of a population presented in number form as statistics. The study and use of demographics often involve simple arithmetic and algebra. Who uses demographics, and what are they used for?

Marketing research is one field that relies on demographics. Marketing research analysts gather statistics for companies that make products or provide services. The companies then use the information to make decisions about new products or services the population may desire. Analysts must know what statistics to use and what to conclude from them. They often focus their information-gathering on a certain age group or gender they think are likely to buy a company's new products or services.

Advertisers who sell a company's products or services use marketing research demographics to study the buying habits of a certain group. They look for demographic information about the group's income, what percentage of the group owns a similar product, where the group gets most of its information, and so on. From these statistics, advertisers speculate about the kind of advertising that will be needed to sell the company's product or service.

1. **Recognizing Words in Context**

   Find the word *speculate* in the passage. One definition below is closest to the meaning of that word. One definition has the opposite or nearly the opposite meaning. The remaining definition has a completely different meaning. Label the definitions C for *closest*, O for *opposite or nearly opposite*, and D for *different*.

   _____ a. think deeply

   _____ b. give passing thought

   _____ c. make a statement

2. **Distinguishing Fact from Opinion**

   Two of the statements below present *facts*, which can be proved. The other statement is an *opinion*, which expresses someone's thoughts or beliefs. Label the statements F for *fact* and O for *opinion*.

   _____ a. Advertisers depend too much on marketing research.

   _____ b. Demographics are presented as statistics.

   _____ c. Marketing research relies on demographics.

3. Keeping Events in Order

Number the statements below 1, 2, and 3 to show the order in which the events should take place.

_____ a. Marketing research analysts study the buying habits of a certain group.

_____ b. The company uses the information to make decisions on new products or services.

_____ c. Advertisers create an advertising strategy.

4. Making Correct Inferences

Two of the statements below are correct *inferences,* or reasonable guesses. They are based on information in the passage. The other statement is an incorrect, or faulty, inference. Label the statements C for *correct* inference and F for *faulty* inference.

_____ a. Different marketing research analysts studying the same group for the same reason are likely to get the same results.

_____ b. An electronic game company will want analysts to find statistics about young people.

_____ c. The mathematics of demography mainly involves averages and percentages.

5. Understanding Main Ideas

One of the statements below expresses the main idea of the passage. One statement is too general, or too broad. The other explains only part of the passage; it is too narrow. Label the statements M for *main idea,* B for *too broad,* and N for *too narrow.*

_____ a. Companies make business decisions based on demographics.

_____ b. Demography is the study of human population.

_____ c. Marketing research analysts gather statistics for companies that make products or provide services.

Correct Answers, Part A _____

Correct Answers, Part B _____

Total Correct Answers _____

Honeymoon in Thailand

Stefan and Cassie chose to spend their honeymoon in Thailand. Neither had ever been overseas, so they were a little concerned about figuring out the currency exchange rate.

When they landed in Bangkok, Stefan and Cassie went to the Thai bank at the airport and converted $500 to 20,500 Thai baht. The exchange rate on that day was 41 baht for every $1 ($500 \times 41 = 20,500$). Stefan and Cassie laughed about how rich they felt holding thousands of Thai baht. But they reminded each other that they must figure out the baht price in relation to dollars before making a purchase. To keep the math calculations simple, they decided to round off that day's exchange rate of 41 to 1 to a number divisible by 10. They chose 40 to 1 as an exchange rate ratio they would use during the whole trip because they knew the exchange rate would change more or less each day.

The bill for dinner that night was 680 baht. They were worried until Stefan worked out how much it would cost them in U.S dollars. They soon discovered they had just eaten a wonderful Thai meal for only about $17 ($680 \div 40 = 17$).

On the last day of their honeymoon, Cassie and Stefan went shopping for gifts. They decided they could spend 5,000 baht, or $125, for gifts. In a store, Cassie saw some beautiful silk scarves that the owner said cost $12 each. Cassie multiplied the exchange rate they were using by the dollar cost to see if she had enough baht to pay for them. She calculated $12 \times 40 = 480$. They were 480 baht each, and she wanted three scarves. Cassie informed Stefan they would have approximately 3,500 baht left if they bought three scarves. (She rounded the cost of each scarf to 500 baht from 480, for a total of 1,500 baht. It was simpler to calculate with 500 than 480.) But Stefan told her the exchange rate was not really 40 to 1. Today it was 45 to 1. They would have to pay more baht today than before. The scarf vendor gave his price in dollars, not baht. Instead of $12 being equivalent to 480 baht (12×40), today $12 was equivalent to 540 baht (12×45). "A few days ago we would have paid 1,440 baht for the three scarves," Stefan said. "But today we will pay 1,620 baht."

Reading Time _____

Recalling Facts

1. The exchange rate when Stefan and Cassie arrived in Thailand was
   - ❏ a. 40 baht for every $1.
   - ❏ b. 41 baht for every $1.
   - ❏ c. $41 for every baht.

2. Stefan and Cassie exchanged _____ at the airport bank.
   - ❏ a. $500
   - ❏ b. $480
   - ❏ c. $1,500

3. Cassie told Stefan they would have approximately _____ left if they bought three scarves.
   - ❏ a. 1,200 baht
   - ❏ b. 3,500 baht
   - ❏ c. $1,500

4. Cassie calculated the cost of the three scarves by first
   - ❏ a. dividing 40 baht by the cost of all three scarves.
   - ❏ b. multiplying 40 baht by the cost of all three scarves.
   - ❏ c. multiplying 40 baht by the cost of one scarf.

5. Stefan knew that the scarves would actually cost more than 480 baht each because
   - ❏ a. the exchange rate was higher than 40 baht.
   - ❏ b. the exchange rate was really 41 baht.
   - ❏ c. the exchange rate would go up by the time they left the store.

Understanding Ideas

6. You can infer from this passage that the currency exchange rate
   - ❏ a. remains the same for weeks or even months at a time.
   - ❏ b. changes regularly.
   - ❏ c. cannot be predicted by banks.

7. You can infer that Stefan and Cassie thought $17 for a Thai dinner was
   - ❏ a. a good deal.
   - ❏ b. pretty expensive.
   - ❏ c. about what they expected.

8. Once Cassie rounded up the cost of the one scarf to 500, she then had to
   - ❏ a. add 500 and 3.
   - ❏ b. divide 500 by 3.
   - ❏ c. multiply 500 by 3.

9. Which of the following statements is *not* true?
   - ❏ a. If the vendor had given them the cost in baht, Cassie would have thought each scarf cost more than $12.
   - ❏ b. The cost of each scarf was more than $12 at that day's exchange rate.
   - ❏ c. Cassie calculated using the 40 baht to $1 exchange rate.

10. One can conclude that the scarf vendor
    - ❏ a. should have given the price of the scarves in baht instead of dollars.
    - ❏ b. will make more money for his scarves today than yesterday.
    - ❏ c. had raised the price of the scarves.

The Euro

On January 1, 2002, the 12 European countries that make up what is currently known as the euro area could no longer use their own currencies. They had a new single currency called the euro (€). It represented high hopes for fostering economic and political cooperation among the countries of the euro area and those of the European Union.

The euro had been introduced three years earlier, in 1999, before the banknote itself was established. Banks and governments began trading electronically at the exchange rate of €1 for every $1.18. That means that in early 1999, a bank exchange rate on $100 in the euro area would return only about €85 ($100 \div 1.18 = 84.75$). However, the exchange value had changed to about €1 for every $1.11 by January 1, 2002, the day the currency was issued. That means that the dollar had grown closer in value to the euro. If your friend from a euro area country had sent you €100 on that day, you would have exchanged it for $7 less than back in 1999 ($100 \times 1.11 = 111$; $118 - 111 = 7$).

The introduction of the euro was a defining event for the countries of the euro area and its trading partners. It was the largest monetary changeover in history.

1. **Recognizing Words in Context**

   Find the word *fostering* in the passage. One definition below is closest to the meaning of that word. One definition has the opposite or nearly the opposite meaning. The remaining definition has a completely different meaning. Label the definitions C for *closest,* O for *opposite or nearly opposite,* and D for *different.*

   _____ a. disheartening

   _____ b. encouraging

   _____ c. changing

2. **Distinguishing Fact from Opinion**

   Two of the statements below present *facts,* which can be proved. The other statement is an *opinion,* which expresses someone's thoughts or beliefs. Label the statements F for *fact* and O for *opinion.*

   _____ a. The value of €1 was worth more than $1 on the first day the euro currency was used in 2002.

   _____ b. The euro area consisted of 12 countries in 2002.

   _____ c. Euro area countries gave up too much by allowing their own currency to become out-of-date.

3. Keeping Events in Order

Two of the statements below describe events that happen at the same time. the other statement describes an event that happens before or after those events. Label them S for *same time*, B for *before*, and A for *after*.

_____ a. People use the euro for the first time.

_____ b. Euros are traded electronically by banks and governments.

_____ c. Citizens of euro area countries stop using their own currencies.

4. Making Correct Inferences

Two of the statements below are correct *inferences*, or reasonable guesses. They are based on information in the passage. The other statement is an incorrect, or faulty, inference. Label the statements C for *correct* inference and F for *faulty* inference.

_____ a. Many citizens of euro area countries wanted to continue using their former currencies.

_____ b. The euro would be considered weak as compared to the dollar if the exchange value changed to €1 for every $1.50.

_____ c. Before 2002 people in the euro area could not use euros even though governments were trading euros electronically.

5. Understanding Main Ideas

One of the statements below expresses the main idea of the passage. One statement is too general, or too broad. The other explains only part of the passage; it is too narrow. Label the statements M for *main idea*, B for *too broad*, and N for *too narrow*.

_____ a. Banks and governments began trading euros electronically before the euro currency was issued.

_____ b. After years of preparation, the euro currency has established itself on the world economy.

_____ c. The euro represented high hopes for cooperation among euro area and EU countries.

Correct Answers, Part A _____

Correct Answers, Part B _____

Total Correct Answers _____

The Impact of the U.S. Census on Congressional Districts

Every 10 years the United States Census report sets the number of representatives for each state in the U.S. House of Representatives. Seats in the House are given to state representatives based on the state's population. Each state is guaranteed one seat in the House. States with larger populations receive additional seats. States are divided into congressional districts. Each member of the House from any given state represents one congressional district.

In 1911 Congress passed a law setting the total number of representatives at 435. The size of a congressional district in 1911 was more than 200,000 people. Since then, the size of each district has grown by about 300 percent. Today each district represents more than 600,000 people. Because the number of seats is limited, a state may lose a seat simply because it is not growing as quickly as another state.

The results of the 2000 Census led to changes in the number of state representatives in 18 states. Ten states lost a total of 12 seats. Eight states gained those 12 seats, keeping the total number of seats at 435. North Carolina secured the last available seat by a very small margin. The state gained one seat and increased its total to 13 representatives. Utah narrowly missed getting this last seat by just 856 people. In the end, the number of seats in Utah did not change.

When a state gains or loses a congressional seat, state lawmakers must redraw district lines. Law dictates that the new districts must be compact and of equal size. Think of an imaginary state with five congressional districts. Each district has 100 people for a total of 500 people. A new Census report, however, results in the loss of one representative and therefore one district. Instead of five congressional districts, the state will have only four. State lawmakers must redraw the districts so that they are equal in size. They divide the population of 500 by 4 to equal 125 people per district.

Redistricting is a complex process, and political parties often influence the outcome. Sometimes politicians redraw the lines in a way that benefits their party. This is called gerrymandering. They may redraw the districts so as to spread voters for the opposing party equally among all the districts. As a result, there would not be enough opposing voters in any one district to win a seat at election time.

Reading Time _____

Recalling Facts

1. The number of representatives for each state in the House of Representatives is set by
   - ❑ a. the Constitution.
   - ❑ b. the U.S. Census report.
   - ❑ c. the president.

2. The total number of representatives in the House is
   - ❑ a. 435.
   - ❑ b. 100.
   - ❑ c. 24.

3. Law dictates that congressional districts must be
   - ❑ a. redrawn every two years.
   - ❑ b. made up of voters from the same political party.
   - ❑ c. compact and of equal size.

4. Gerrymandering occurs when politicians
   - ❑ a. petition for additional seats in Congress.
   - ❑ b. redraw district lines to benefit their party.
   - ❑ c. slow the process of redistricting to avoid losing seats in Congress.

5. Each state is guaranteed
   - ❑ a. one seat in the House of Representatives.
   - ❑ b. two seats in the House of Representatives.
   - ❑ c. five seats in the House of Representatives.

Understanding Ideas

6. A state is likely to gain an additional seat in the House of Representatives if its population has
   - ❑ a. increased.
   - ❑ b. decreased.
   - ❑ c. remained the same.

7. One can conclude from the passage that the U.S. Census measures a state's
   - ❑ a. income.
   - ❑ b. crime rate.
   - ❑ c. population.

8. One can conclude that congressional redistricting occurs as a result of
   - ❑ a. annual population changes.
   - ❑ b. a state's gain or loss of a congressional seat.
   - ❑ c. political campaigns.

9. One can infer that if 8 states lose a total of 10 congressional seats after a new census, then the total number of seats gained by other states is
   - ❑ a. 5.
   - ❑ b. 10.
   - ❑ c. 20.

10. One can infer that if the population decreased in a state with one congressional district, the district would
    - ❑ a. lose its congressional seat.
    - ❑ b. need to redraw its lines.
    - ❑ c. not be affected in Congress.

3   B   Does the Majority Rule?

Thomas Jefferson wrote in 1800, "The voice of the majority decides."
Many principles of U.S. government depend on majority rule. For example,
a bill can become law only if more than 50 percent of each house of
Congress passes the bill. It must receive a majority of the vote in each
house. There are 435 representatives and 100 senators; for the bill to pass,
218 representatives and 51 senators would have to vote for it.

Majority rule is only one way in which matters of law and government
are decided, however. Some decisions in Congress require a two-thirds vote.
If the president vetoes a bill that Congress has passed, the bill can become
law only if it passes both houses again—but this time by a two-thirds vote
in each house. In order to make such a bill a law, 290 representatives
(435 × ⅔) and 67 senators (100 × ⅔) would have to vote for it.

Some matters are decided by less than a majority vote. Most elections
with more than two candidates are decided by a plurality. The candidate
who receives the highest number of votes wins, even if this number is not a
majority.

1. **Recognizing Words in Context**

   Find the word *majority* in the passage.
   One definition below is closest to the
   meaning of that word. One definition
   has the opposite or nearly the
   opposite meaning. The remaining
   definition has a completely different
   meaning. Label the definitions C for
   closest, O for *opposite or nearly opposite*,
   and D for *different*.

   _____ a. less than half

   _____ b. two-thirds

   _____ c. more than half

2. **Distinguishing Fact from Opinion**

   Two of the statements below present
   facts, which can be proved. The
   other statement is an *opinion*, which
   expresses someone's thoughts or
   beliefs. Label the statements F for
   fact and O for *opinion*.

   _____ a. Elections should be
   decided by a majority vote.

   _____ b. A bill can become law only
   if a majority of each house
   votes for it.

   _____ c. The president has the right
   to veto a bill that Congress
   has passed.

3. **Keeping Events in Order**

   Number the statements below 1, 2, and 3 to show the procedure by which a bill becomes a law.

   _____ a. The president vetoes the bill.

   _____ b. Congress passes the bill by a two-thirds vote.

   _____ c. Congress passes the bill by majority vote.

4. **Making Correct Inferences**

   Two of the statements below are correct *inferences,* or reasonable guesses. They are based on information in the passage. The other statement is an incorrect, or faulty, inference. Label the statements C for *correct* inference and F for *faulty* inference.

   _____ a. To win by plurality requires more than half of the vote.

   _____ b. If the President does not veto a bill passed by Congress, the bill becomes law.

   _____ c. Most matters are not decided by a two-thirds vote.

5. **Understanding Main Ideas**

   One of the statements below expresses the main idea of the passage. One statement is too general, or too broad. The other explains only part of the passage; it is too narrow. Label the statements M for *main idea,* B for *too broad,* and N for *too narrow.*

   _____ a. Majority rule is just one way in which matters of law and government are decided.

   _____ b. Elections are often decided by a plurality.

   _____ c. Majority rule is a principle of democracy.

Correct Answers, Part A _____

Correct Answers, Part B _____

Total Correct Answers _____

What Is Calculus?

Calculus is a branch of mathematics that studies continuously changing quantities. Its development is credited to two late 17th-century mathematicians, Gottfried Leibniz and Isaac Newton. Calculus is more or less a combination of algebra and geometry. If you are familiar with either algebra or geometry, gaining an understanding of what calculus involves should not be too difficult.

Many scholars refer to calculus as the "mathematics of change." Algebra or geometry can be applied to problems that include consistent factors. But problems that involve changing circumstances require calculus. There are many branches of calculus, but the two main ones are integral calculus and differential calculus.

Integral calculus is applied in finding values such as area and volume. If you need to compute the square feet in a rectangle of land, you would use multiplication: length × width. On the other hand, if you want to find the square footage of an oval of land, you would need to use integral calculus. Integral calculus would also be useful in finding the amount of air in a balloon or the amount of water in a pail. If there is some change in dimensions such as length or width and the rate of that change is known, integral calculus will help solve the problem. Differential calculus is used to find rates of change in the grade of a slope or a curve.

Mathematicians typically use a combination of integral and differential calculus in solving their problems. Let's look at an example. Imagine that you need to push a box up a hill on a smooth, consistent incline. If you push with an unchanging force, your pace would be consistent. Using some traditional algebra, you can compute the amount of energy needed to move the box up the hill. However, let's say the vertical height of the hill had changed. Calculus would help you compute the change in the height of the hill. You could then find the amount of energy needed to get to the top.

Another example could involve scoring a point in a basketball game. Let's say you score a point while crossing the court in a semicircular move. Your distance from the net would vary with each second of movement in that semicircle. So how far did you actually shoot the ball to score that winning point? Applying calculus to some detailed drawings of your game strategy could help you determine distances within your constantly changing positions.

Reading Time _____

Recalling Facts

1. *Calculus* is a branch of mathematics that studies
   - ❏ a. changing quantities.
   - ❏ b. unchanging force and pace.
   - ❏ c. geometry and multiplication.

2. Calculus is a combination of
   - ❏ a. area and volume.
   - ❏ b. geometry and algebra.
   - ❏ c. multiplication and division.

3. Differential calculus
   - ❏ a. is the same as integral calculus.
   - ❏ b. studies difference in numbers.
   - ❏ c. studies rates of change.

4. Integral calculus is used to measure
   - ❏ a. area or volume.
   - ❏ b. length.
   - ❏ c. change.

5. Integral calculus can be used for problems involving change when
   - ❏ a. the rate of change is known.
   - ❏ b. the rate of change must be computed.
   - ❏ c. change occurs only once.

Understanding Ideas

6. One might infer from this passage that integral calculus solves problems involving
   - ❏ a. algebra but not geometry.
   - ❏ b. changes in the slope of a hill.
   - ❏ c. changes within an area of land.

7. Calculus would *not* be useful for
   - ❏ a. computing the gallons of water in a standard rectangular aquarium.
   - ❏ b. finding the square footage of a domed roof.
   - ❏ c. finding the length of overhead cable television wires.

8. Mathematicians would use a combination of integral and differential calculus to solve a problem involving
   - ❏ a. the area and volume of an egg.
   - ❏ b. the area and volume of a drum.
   - ❏ c. the area and volume of a soccer ball.

9. People who work with _____ figures would be likely to use calculus.
   - ❏ a. one-dimensional
   - ❏ b. two-dimensional
   - ❏ c. three-dimensional

10. One can conclude that
    - ❏ a. people who can learn algebra and geometry can learn calculus.
    - ❏ b. calculus deals more with ideas than with real situations.
    - ❏ c. any math problem can be solved with calculus.

Gottfried Leibniz

Gottfried Leibniz was born in 1646 in Germany. He was a scientist and a mathematician. Leibniz invented the first mechanical calculator that could perform multiplication and division. He also invented a new form of binary number system that is used today in digital computers. Leibniz, along with Sir Isaac Newton, is credited with the development of modern calculus. Newton believed that there are limits to the exactness of solutions gained by using calculus. But Leibniz believed that the possibilities for more detailed solutions through calculus are infinite, or without end, in many uses.

Leibniz is often acknowledged as the first to use the term *function* in calculus. He used it to describe a quantity such as a curve's slope at a specific point on that curve. The term has taken on more meaning since Leibniz first described it in 1694. In calculus many real-life problems are studied by expressing one quantity as a function of another.

In the 1670s, Leibniz presented his idea of infinitesimal calculus. The word *infinitesimal* means "too small to be measured." It deals with functions when the values of their variable expressions come close to zero. In 1675 Leibniz was the first to demonstrate integral calculus. Many of the symbols he introduced then are still in use.

1. **Recognizing Words in Context**

   Find the word *acknowledged* in the passage. One definition below is closest to the meaning of that word. One definition has the opposite or nearly the opposite meaning. The remaining definition has a completely different meaning. Label the definitions C for *closest*, O for *opposite or nearly opposite*, and D for *different*.

   _____ a. recognized

   _____ b. rejected

   _____ c. followed

2. **Distinguishing Fact from Opinion**

   Two of the statements below present *facts*, which can be proved. The other statement is an *opinion*, which expresses someone's thoughts or beliefs. Label the statements F for *fact* and O for *opinion*.

   _____ a. Leibniz's ideas are still used by mathematicians.

   _____ b. Leibniz and Newton both contributed to modern calculus.

   _____ c. Leibniz was the most important mathematician of the 17th century.

3. **Keeping Events in Order**

Number the statements below 1, 2, and 3 to show the order in which they occurred in Leibniz's life.

_____ a. Leibniz demonstrated integral calculus.

_____ b. Leibniz presented his theory of infinitesimal calculus.

_____ c. Leibniz introduced the term *function*.

4. **Making Correct Inferences**

Two of the statements below are correct *inferences*, or reasonable guesses. They are based on information in the passage. The other statement is an incorrect, or faulty, inference. Label the statements C for *correct* inference and F for *faulty* inference.

_____ a. The term *function* as it is used in calculus today came from the idea presented by Leibniz.

_____ b. Leibniz's theory of infinitesimal calculus could deal with functions that have smaller and smaller variable expressions.

_____ c. Leibniz's theories of infinitesimal calculus agreed with the ideas of Isaac Newton.

5. **Understanding Main Ideas**

One of the statements below expresses the main idea of the passage. One statement is too general, or too broad. The other explains only part of the passage; it is too narrow. Label the statements M for *main idea*, B for *too broad*, and N for *too narrow*.

_____ a. Gottfried Leibniz was an important influence on modern calculus.

_____ b. Gottfried Leibniz introduced the ideas of infinitesimal and integral calculus.

_____ c. Gottfried Leibniz's binary number system is used in today's computers.

Correct Answers, Part A _____

Correct Answers, Part B _____

Total Correct Answers _____

The Special Theory of Relativity

Albert Einstein introduced his Special Theory of Relativity in 1905. This theory changed our understanding of the relationships between time, motion, and space.

Prior to Einstein's theory, people believed that space and time were constant—they never altered. Under no circumstances would a 12-inch ruler be longer or shorter than 12 inches. Time also was constant; a person's *perception* of time could change—think how "time flies" when you are having fun—but time itself would not change.

Einstein realized, however, that the only constant in nature is the speed of light. Time can go faster or slower, and space can expand or contract, but the speed of light never changes. The speed of light is always 186,282 miles per second, regardless of the speed of the source of the light.

Here is a way to visualize the relationship between time and the speed of light. You must remember, however, that human vision depends on light. What we call *sight* is an image carried from an object to our eyes on light waves going 186,282 miles per hour.

As you leave school on the bus, the clock on the school's clock tower reads 3:00. As the bus leaves the school at 30 miles per hour, you watch time on the clock change to 3:01; your wristwatch also shows 3:01.

Now imagine you get on the Special Relativity bus, which travels at the speed of light. As you leave the school, the clock on the clock tower reads 3:00. One minute later it still shows 3:00. After five minutes, it's still 3:00.

Remember the connection between light and sight? Light that transmits the message "3:00" to your eyes is going the same speed as the bus. At 186,262 miles per second, the message "3:00" stays with you on the bus. Even on the Special Relativity bus, however, your wristwatch would show 3:01 after one minute and 3:05 after five minutes.

So is time standing still or not? Well, it's all relative.

Einstein realized that time and space are *relative* to the speed of light. If you are moving at an accelerated rate of speed relative to the clock—or if the clock is moving at an accelerated rate of speed relative to you—time will slow down. The faster you move, the slower time will go—until it seems to stop entirely when you reach the speed of light.

Reading Time _____

Recalling Facts

1. The Special Theory of Relativity deals with the way we understand
   - ❏ a. vision, taste, and sound.
   - ❏ b. clocks, wristwatches, and timers.
   - ❏ c. time, motion, and space.

2. According to Einstein, the only constant in nature is
   - ❏ a. the speed of light.
   - ❏ b. the passing of time.
   - ❏ c. the size of space.

3. Light travels at a speed of
   - ❏ a. 186,282 miles per hour.
   - ❏ b. 186,282 miles per minute.
   - ❏ c. 186,282 miles per second.

4. Which of the following is needed for human vision?
   - ❏ a. motion
   - ❏ b. light
   - ❏ c. time

5. If you travel close to the speed of light,
   - ❏ a. time seems to slow down.
   - ❏ b. time seems to speed up.
   - ❏ c. time doesn't seem to change.

Understanding Ideas

6. One can conclude from this passage that motion
   - ❏ a. increases the speed of light.
   - ❏ b. decreases the speed of light.
   - ❏ c. has no effect on the speed of light.

7. According to this article, the passage of time would be different for a person standing next to the clock tower and a person
   - ❏ a. traveling on a bus at normal speed.
   - ❏ b. traveling on a bus at the speed of light.
   - ❏ c. having a wonderful time.

8. According to this passage, there is a difference between
   - ❏ a. the measurement of time and the perception of time.
   - ❏ b. the speed of light and the speed of time.
   - ❏ c. the measurement of distance and the passage of time.

9. This passage explores the relationship between
   - ❏ a. speed and time.
   - ❏ b. light and sight.
   - ❏ c. space and time.

10. This article suggests that before Einstein,
    - ❏ a. no one understood the nature of time, motion, or space.
    - ❏ b. scientists had a different understanding of the relationships between time, motion, and space.
    - ❏ c. there was no scientific understanding of the natural world.

Professor Mallett's Time Machine

The African American scientist Ronald Mallett grew up in New York City's South Bronx. His father died suddenly of a heart attack when young Ronald was only 10 years old. It was during this sad time that he read about the idea of time travel in H.G. Wells's fantastic tale, *The Time Machine*. The boy imagined building such a machine and traveling back in time to see his father.

Mallet went on to earn his Ph.D. in physics from Pennsylvania State University. Today he is a professor of physics at the University of Connecticut. His study of Einstein's theories of relativity has persuaded him that time travel may one day be possible.

Einstein suggested that space and time are not separate systems. They form a single elastic fabric called *space-time*. This elastic, curving fabric allows time to run concurrently at different speeds, and it allows the same distance to be at once both long and short. Mallett has designed a device that uses a beam of light from a laser to twist this fabric until the future comes around behind the past in a continuous spiral. In the loops of this spiral, there is no beginning and no end. Mallett's idea is to create this spiral and devise a way for a human being to enter it and move backward and forward through time.

1. **Recognizing Words in Context**

   Find the word *concurrently* in the passage. One definition below is closest to the meaning of that word. One definition has the opposite or nearly the opposite meaning. The remaining definition has a completely different meaning. Label the definitions C for *closest*, O for *opposite or nearly opposite*, and D for *different*.

   _____ a. at different moments

   _____ b. at the same time

   _____ c. side by side

2. **Distinguishing Fact from Opinion**

   Two of the statements below present *facts*, which can be proved. The other statement is an *opinion*, which expresses someone's thoughts or beliefs. Label the statements F for *fact* and O for *opinion*.

   _____ a. Mallett found H.G. Wells's *The Time Machine* to be thought provoking.

   _____ b. Time travel may one day be possible.

   _____ c. Mallett is trying to solve the problem of time travel.

3. Keeping Events in Order

Number the statements below 1, 2, and 3 to show the order in which the events took place.

_____ a. Mallett discovered Einstein's theories of relativity.

_____ b. Mallett began teaching physics at the University of Connecticut.

_____ c. Mallett read H.G. Wells's *The Time Machine.*

4. Making Correct Inferences

Two of the statements below are correct *inferences,* or reasonable guesses. They are based on information in the passage. The other statement is an incorrect, or faulty, inference. Label the statements C for *correct* inference and F for *faulty* inference.

_____ a. Professor Mallett expects to travel back through time and see his father.

_____ b. H.G. Wells's *The Time Machine* inspired Mallett to study science.

_____ c. The beam of light from a laser is extremely powerful.

5. Understanding Main Ideas

One of the statements below expresses the main idea of the passage. One statement is too general, or too broad. The other explains only part of the passage; it is too narrow. Label the statements M for *main idea,* B for *too broad,* and N for *too narrow.*

_____ a. Ronald Mallett turned a boyhood tragedy into a career in science.

_____ b. Professor Mallet has designed a device that could be a time machine.

_____ c. The idea of time travel has interested many people for a long time.

Correct Answers, Part A _____

Correct Answers, Part B _____

Total Correct Answers _____

What Is Pi?

Neil designs landscapes. One of his drawings calls for a circle filled with flowers. Neil must figure out how many flowers he needs to fill the circle. He uses the formula for finding the area of a circle: area equals pi times the square of the radius ($A = \pi r^2$). Pi, pronounced like "pie" and represented by the Greek letter π, is always used in formulas that involve the measurement of circles. The radius of Neil's circle, or the distance from the center of the circle to its outer edge, represents 6 feet in the garden. Six feet squared is 36 feet. Neil multiplies 36×3.1416 (pi) to get 113.0976, or a little more than 113 square feet of flowers.

The need to measure the area of a circle drove ancient scholars to discover pi. Pi is the ratio of the circumference of a circle to its diameter. The circumference is the distance around a circle. The diameter of a circle is the length of a straight line through the center of the circle. So $\pi = 3.14$ means that the circumference of a circle is a little more than three times longer than the diameter. Pi is always the same number no matter the size of the circle. Pi is an irrational number, which means it has an infinite sequence of nonrepeating digits to the right of the decimal point. For most everyday uses, though, people just round off pi to 3.1416, or even 3.14.

People of ancient Babylon and Egypt first discovered pi more than 4,000 years ago. Many centuries later, the Greeks studied pi. The Greeks determined how to compute the area of polygons (closed figures with more than two sides) such as squares and triangles. The Greek scholar Archimedes studied circles by placing polygons inside and outside circles and then computing the difference between their areas. In this way, he was able to define the approximate value of the ratio of circumference to diameter as $211,875 \div 67,441$, or 3.14163. This mathematical constant was used for hundreds of years before it was named. In 1706 mathematician William Jones first named the constant *pi* and used the symbol π to represent it. Pi is the Greek letter that begins the word meaning to "measure around."

Pi has been used in many fields of study. Math and science formulas include pi to form the basis of work in fields such as architecture, construction, engineering, electronics, and computer science.

Reading Time _____

Recalling Facts

1. The value of pi is often expressed as
   - ❑ a. r^2.
   - ❑ b. 3.1416.
   - ❑ c. 113.0976.

2. Pi is defined as the ratio of the
   - ❑ a. circumference of a circle to its diameter.
   - ❑ b. circumference of a circle to its radius.
   - ❑ c. circumference of a circle to its area.

3. Pi is
   - ❑ a. a variable.
   - ❑ b. an irrational number.
   - ❑ c. a rational number.

4. The _____ is the distance around a circle.
   - ❑ a. circumference
   - ❑ b. radius
   - ❑ c. diameter

5. The best-known study of pi was done by the
   - ❑ a. Egyptians.
   - ❑ b. Babylonians.
   - ❑ c. Greeks.

Understanding Ideas

6. From the information in the passage, one can conclude that pi
   - ❑ a. could be used to find the area of a circle of any size.
   - ❑ b. is used only by scientists.
   - ❑ c. was more important in ancient times than it is today.

7. One can conclude from the information in the passage that
   - ❑ a. the diameter of a circle is three times the length of the radius.
   - ❑ b. the circumference is twice the length of the diameter.
   - ❑ c. the radius is half the length of the diameter.

8. Which person would be likely to use pi most often?
   - ❑ a. a musician
   - ❑ b. a landscape designer
   - ❑ c. a cook

9. Considering the passage, one can conclude that ancient scholars thought that
   - ❑ a. circles were less difficult to measure than polygons.
   - ❑ b. circles were more difficult to measure than polygons.
   - ❑ c. circles and polygons were equally difficult to measure.

10. From the passage, one can conclude that rounding pi to a few decimal places
    - ❑ a. was made easier by computers.
    - ❑ b. makes pi easier to work with.
    - ❑ c. has rarely been attempted.

Archimedes (287–212 B.C.E.) was a Greek scholar whose work surpassed that of any other mathematician for hundreds of years. He discovered that the ratio between the circumference of a circle and its diameter was a constant. This ratio, known as pi, is also known as "Archimedes' constant." Archimedes' extensive contributions to mathematics have been applied to the fields of science and engineering.

The ancient Greeks had a limited understanding of numbers and believed that no number was greater than 10,000. Archimedes invented a system to write numbers up to 10^{64}, which is 1 followed by 64 zeros. He also laid the foundation for a method of calculation known today as calculus. Archimedes was the first person to study spirals, and he expanded existing knowledge of spheres and cylinders. He proved that the volume of a sphere is two-thirds of the volume of a cylinder that surrounds it. He was so proud of this proof that he chose it for his tombstone.

Beyond his work in math, Archimedes discovered the principles of density and buoyancy. These principles explain why wood floats on water, while solid metal sinks. His inventions include the lever and the pulley. It is said that he was drawing math diagrams in the sand when he died.

1. **Recognizing Words in Context**

   Find the word *extensive* in the passage. One definition below is closest to the meaning of that word. One definition has the opposite or nearly the opposite meaning. The remaining definition has a completely different meaning. Label the definitions C for *closest*, O for *opposite or nearly opposite*, and D for *different*.

   _____ a. narrow

   _____ b. out of order

   _____ c. far-reaching

2. **Distinguishing Fact from Opinion**

   Two of the statements below present *facts*, which can be proved. The other statement is an *opinion*, which expresses someone's thoughts or beliefs. Label the statements F for *fact* and O for *opinion*.

   _____ a. Archimedes was history's greatest mathematician.

   _____ b. Archimedes invented the lever and the pulley.

   _____ c. Archimedes discovered the principles of density and buoyancy.

3. Keeping Events in Order

Number the statements below 1, 2, and 3 to show the order in which the events took place.

_____ a. One of Archimedes' formulas was written on his tombstone.

_____ b. Archimedes proved that the ratio between the circumference of a circle and its diameter was a constant.

_____ c. The ancient Greeks defined infinity as 10,000.

4. Making Correct Inferences

Two of the statements below are correct *inferences,* or reasonable guesses. They are based on information in the passage. The other statement is an incorrect, or faulty, inference. Label the statements C for *correct* inference and F for *faulty* inference.

_____ a. Archimedes had wide-ranging interests.

_____ b. Some of Archimedes' inventions are used today.

_____ c. Archimedes saw only purely scientific uses for pi.

5. Understanding Main Ideas

One of the statements below expresses the main idea of the passage. One statement is too general, or too broad. The other explains only part of the passage; it is too narrow. Label the statements M for *main idea,* B for *too broad,* and N for *too narrow.*

_____ a. Archimedes' discoveries helped advance science, mathematics, and engineering.

_____ b. Archimedes calculated the volume of a sphere.

_____ c. Greek mathematicians such as Archimedes made many discoveries.

Correct Answers, Part A _____

Correct Answers, Part B _____

Total Correct Answers _____

The NBA Salary Cap

The high salaries of professional athletes have been the subject of some debate. Some people think professional athletes are paid too much for "playing a game." Others think they should be paid the same as other popular entertainers.

The National Basketball Association (NBA) uses a salary cap to keep its players' salaries at a certain level. The salary cap is the maximum dollar amount each NBA team can spend on its players for the season. In 1983 the salary cap was put into effect to ensure that no team could offer a player more money than any other team could. This way all teams had the same chance to get the best players.

Setting the amount of the salary cap for each season begins with the calculation of the teams' Basketball Related Income (BRI). The BRI is the total income for all the NBA teams. The salary cap, subject to certain adjustments, is calculated by multiplying each team's BRI by 48.04 percent, subtracting players' benefits, and then dividing the result by the number of teams.

Even after the salary cap was put in place, teams found ways around it. Teams that could afford to pay high salaries for players continued to do so. Some teams that did not make as much money as other teams were finding it hard to attract good players.

In 2001 the NBA was still struggling with the issue of high salaries. The league came up with a plan in which not more than 10 percent of each player's paycheck went into a special account. If players' salaries for that year exceeded 55 percent of the BRI, the amount over that limit was given to the team owners. The rest went to the players. If salaries didn't exceed 55 percent, the players had all their money returned to them.

Another way that the league has tried to keep salaries close to equal among teams is with the so-called luxury tax. In this plan, teams may overspend on players' salaries, but if *all* players' salaries do not exceed a certain percentage of the BRI, then no team has to pay the luxury tax. In 2002–2003, players' salaries did exceed the limit. So, each of the 29 teams that went over 61 percent of the BRI was charged a dollar for every dollar they were over. Teams that had stayed under the limit enjoyed a share of the tax money.

Reading Time _____

Recalling Facts

1. The NBA salary cap
   - ❏ a. is a percentage of salary set by the league.
   - ❏ b. rules that teams must pay a tax.
   - ❏ c. keeps players' salaries at a certain level.

2. Basketball Related Income (BRI) is
   - ❏ a. money from NBA ticket sales.
   - ❏ b. revenue from NBA television broadcasts.
   - ❏ c. the total income for all the NBA teams.

3. The salary cap is calculated by multiplying each team's BRI by _____ and then dividing the result by the number of teams.
   - ❏ a. 48.04 percent
   - ❏ b. 55 percent
   - ❏ c. 61 percent

4. In 2001 the NBA came up with a plan in which
   - ❏ a. 55 percent of a player's paycheck was taxed.
   - ❏ b. 10 percent of each player's paycheck went into a special account.
   - ❏ c. players' salaries had to exceed 55 percent of the BRI.

5. Besides the salary cap, another way that the league has tried to keep salaries close to equal among teams is
   - ❏ a. through the BRI.
   - ❏ b. with the luxury tax.
   - ❏ c. by allowing teams to pay high salaries for players.

Understanding Ideas

6. According to the passage, why did the luxury tax have to be paid in 2002–2003?
   - ❏ a. Salaries were 55 percent of BRI.
   - ❏ b. Teams earned too much money.
   - ❏ c. Salaries exceeded 61 percent of the BRI.

7. What is one reason why the NBA sets a salary cap for players?
   - ❏ a. The NBA believes teams will become too wealthy.
   - ❏ b. The NBA believes all players should be paid the same amount.
   - ❏ c. Some teams can afford to pay more for players than other teams can.

8. The NBA luxury tax plan states that if all players' salaries
   - ❏ a. do not exceed a percentage of the BRI, then no team has to pay the luxury tax.
   - ❏ b. exceed a percentage of the BRI, then every team has to pay the luxury tax.
   - ❏ c. do not exceed a percentage of the BRI, then every team is paid a luxury tax.

9. Which teams must pay the luxury tax?
   - ❏ a. only the teams that exceed a percentage of the BRI
   - ❏ b. all the teams if only one team exceeds a percentage of the BRI
   - ❏ c. none of the teams if all the teams exceed a percentage of the BRI

10. One can conclude that as long as the BRI goes up, the salary cap will
    - ❏ a. go down.
    - ❏ b. go up.
    - ❏ c. no longer be needed.

NBA Minimum Salary Practices

The NBA and the Players Association have tried to keep costs under control. They signed an agreement stipulating that salaries should have a minimum and a maximum. Both the low-end and high-end salaries are based on the number of years a player has been in the league. A player who has been in the league for five years gets paid at a figure somewhere between the minimum and the maximum for five-year players.

That's where it stops being simple. A team may want to sign a 10-year veteran player for the remainder of the season at the minimum salary. But the team may not be able to pay the 10-year minimum salary even for someone who is going to play only part of a year. According to the agreement, the team will pay the player at the minimum salary level for a four-year veteran, and the league will pay the rest.

The minimum salary for a four-year veteran in 2004–2005 was $745,046. So a 10-year veteran with a minimum-salary contract of $1,100,000 would be paid $745,046 by his team. The league would then pick up the $354,954 balance.

The reason is simple. The players and the league want well-known, veteran players to keep playing—as long as someone is willing to pay them.

1. **Recognizing Words in Context**

   Find the word *stipulating* in the passage. One definition below is closest to the meaning of that word. One definition has the opposite or nearly the opposite meaning. The remaining definition has a completely different meaning. Label the definitions C for *closest,* O for *opposite or nearly opposite,* and D for *different.*

   _____ a. specifying

   _____ b. uncovering

   _____ c. suggesting

2. **Distinguishing Fact from Opinion**

   Two of the statements below present *facts,* which can be proved. The other statement is an *opinion,* which expresses someone's thoughts or beliefs. Label the statements F for *fact* and O for *opinion.*

   _____ a. With some minimum-salary contracts, the league office pays part of the salary for certain players.

   _____ b. NBA players and team owners try to keep costs under control.

   _____ c. NBA players should be paid much less.

3. Keeping Events in Order

Number the statements below 1, 2, and 3 to show the order in which the events should take place.

_____ a. The team and the league sign an agreement that has a special clause for veteran players.

_____ b. A veteran player signs a minimum-salary contract for a 10-year player.

_____ c. The team and the league each pay a portion of the player's salary.

4. Making Correct Inferences

Two of the statements below are correct *inferences*, or reasonable guesses. They are based on information in the passage. The other statement is an incorrect, or faulty, inference. Label the statements C for *correct* inference and F for *faulty* inference.

_____ a. NBA players are paid according to the number of years they have been in the league.

_____ b. Players with seven years in the NBA are paid within a salary range for seven-year players.

_____ c. A nine-year player on a short contract plays for the minimum salary of a four-year player.

5. Understanding Main Ideas

One of the statements below expresses the main idea of the passage. One statement is too general, or too broad. The other explains only part of the passage; it is too narrow. Label the statements M for *main idea,* B for *too broad,* and N for *too narrow.*

_____ a. A team and the league may sometimes share the cost of the salary for a veteran player.

_____ b. NBA players are paid within a range of salaries based on the number of years they have been in the league.

_____ c. The agreement between the league and the players aims to control costs while providing ways to pay players very well.

Correct Answers, Part A _____

Correct Answers, Part B _____

Total Correct Answers _____

Land Surveyors

Land surveyors measure distances, directions, and angles on the earth's surface. Many years ago, one of a land surveyor's tools for measuring distance was a simple rod. To measure distances, a surveyor would lay the rod down on the ground, flip it end over end, and count the number of rod-lengths. Surveyors today sometimes have to verify boundaries that were once measured in rod-lengths. When this happens, the surveyor has to convert the rod-lengths to feet. This is done by multiplying the length of the rod used by the length of the property as measured in rods.

A theodolite is a modern surveyor's tool for measuring horizontal and vertical angles. It combines the capabilities of a telescope, a ruler, and a protractor. The theodolite has a telescopic lens with a crosshair that allows for seeing great distances with precision. A laser with a specialized prism acts as the "ruler" and provides a method for measuring slope distances. Angle measurements in the horizontal and vertical planes—the "protractor"— are provided by digital readouts.

Surveyors very often measure land that has hills and dips, or that involves many sides. To measure natural landscapes like these, surveyors measure the distances and angles between selected points and then perform calculations. For example, to measure a hill, surveyors must determine the gradient of the hill's slope. Knowledge of trigonometry is necessary for measuring natural landscapes.

Imagine a situation in which a surveyor must measure land whose farthest boundary line is hidden by a thick clump of trees. The surveyor finds the two endpoints of the property line. But because of the trees, the distance between the points cannot be measured. Using the two known endpoints, the surveyor sets up a third point to create a triangle. The distances between the third point and the two known points are then measured, as are the angles. And a simple calculation gives the unknown distance.

New technology continues to change the way the work is done. Computers handle many of the calculations, and CAD (computer-aided design) programs determine boundaries. Surveyors also use a satellite tracking system on many projects. Points on the earth are found using radio signals sent by satellites. To use this system, a surveyor places a signal receiver on a desired point. The receiver collects information from a number of satellites at the same time to find the position.

Reading Time _____

Recalling Facts

1. Land surveyors measure distances, directions, and _____ on the earth's surface.
   - ❑ a. location
   - ❑ b. boundaries
   - ❑ c. angles

2. A rod-length is
   - ❑ a. a measuring tool once used by surveyors.
   - ❑ b. a measurement calculated from feet.
   - ❑ c. the length of a measuring rod once used by surveyors.

3. To measure land with a hill, the surveyor needs to find the
   - ❑ a. gradient of the hill's slope.
   - ❑ b. distance to the top of the hill.
   - ❑ c. distance around the hill.

4. A _____ is a surveyor's tool for measuring horizontal and vertical angles.
   - ❑ a. theodolite
   - ❑ b. protractor
   - ❑ c. prism

5. A laser with a specialized prism acts as a
   - ❑ a. telescope.
   - ❑ b. ruler.
   - ❑ c. satellite tracking system.

Understanding Ideas

6. If two endpoints are known and the third cannot be seen, surveyors first
   - ❑ a. double the known endpoints to create a square.
   - ❑ b. set up a third point to create a triangle.
   - ❑ c. add to the measures of the known endpoints.

7. One could infer that in measuring a distance in which the curve of the earth is a factor, surveyors would use
   - ❑ a. a satellite tracking system.
   - ❑ b. computer-aided design.
   - ❑ c. a theodolite.

8. Which of three functions mentioned as part of the theodolite would be used to measure angles?
   - ❑ a. telescope
   - ❑ b. ruler
   - ❑ c. protractor

9. Which of three functions mentioned as part of the theodolite would be used to measure the slope of a hill?
   - ❑ a. telescope
   - ❑ b. ruler
   - ❑ c. protractor

10. It is likely that the crosshair on the telescopic lens allows for
    - ❑ a. greater precision.
    - ❑ b. seeing great distances.
    - ❑ c. measuring angles in every direction.

Benjamin Banneker: A Self-Made Man

Benjamin Banneker was born in 1731 on a farm near Baltimore, Maryland. He was the son of an enslaved father and a free mother. Banneker learned to read and write from his maternal grandmother. Over several winters, Banneker attended a small school for whites and free blacks where he developed a keen interest in mathematics and science.

Banneker's cleverness and curiosity drove him toward learning what he could on his own. As a young man, Banneker disassembled a pocket watch and studied its mechanism. He then built a wooden clock from a design he had drawn of the watch, using a knife to carve the wheels and gears. The clock kept accurate time for several decades. Over the 20 years that followed, Banneker taught himself mathematics, physics, astronomy, and surveying.

Banneker had a remarkable memory. Around 1789 he was hired to work with a surveying team on a commission to plan the layout of the new capital city, Washington, D.C. Shortly after the team began working, President Washington fired the city's chief planner, who left the country with all of the designs and maps. In two days Banneker reproduced from memory a complete layout of the city, including streets, parks, and major buildings.

When Banneker retired, he was visited by people from all over the world. He died at his farm in 1806.

1. Recognizing Words in Context

Find the word *disassembled* in the passage. One definition below is closest to the meaning of that word. One definition has the opposite or nearly the opposite meaning. The remaining definition has a completely different meaning. Label the definitions C for *closest*, O for *opposite or nearly opposite*, and D for *different*.

_____ a. put together

_____ b. took apart

_____ c. put aside

2. Distinguishing Fact from Opinion

Two of the statements below present *facts*, which can be proved. The other statement is an *opinion*, which expresses someone's thoughts or beliefs. Label the statements F for *fact* and O for *opinion*.

_____ a. Banneker was born on a farm near Baltimore, Maryland.

_____ b. Washington, D.C., should be called Banneker City.

_____ c. Banneker accomplished many things with little formal schooling.

3. Keeping Events in Order

Number the statements below 1, 2, and 3 to show the order in which the events took place.

_____ a. Banneker reproduced a complete layout of the city from memory.

_____ b. The city's designer left with the city's plans and maps.

_____ c. Banneker was hired as a surveyor for the planning of the new capital city.

4. Making Correct Inferences

Two of the statements below are correct *inferences,* or reasonable guesses. They are based on information in the passage. The other statement is an incorrect, or faulty, inference. Label the statements C for *correct* inference and F for *faulty* inference.

_____ a. Banneker's keen memory and strong curiosity were major factors in his success.

_____ b. Banneker did not learn very much at the school he attended.

_____ c. Banneker gained the respect of the members of the Washington, D.C., planning team.

5. Understanding Main Ideas

One of the statements below expresses the main idea of the passage. One statement is too general, or too broad. The other explains only part of the passage; it is too narrow. Label the statements M for *main idea,* B for *too broad,* and N for *too narrow.*

_____ a. Benjamin Banneker was self-taught in science and mathematics.

_____ b. Benjamin Banneker learned how to build a clock from a pocket watch.

_____ c. Benjamin Banneker was successful at many things, mostly through his own efforts.

Correct Answers, Part A _____

Correct Answers, Part B _____

Total Correct Answers _____

The Federal Income Tax

In the United States, federal, state, and local governments can levy a variety of taxes. The most important federal tax is the federal income tax.

The permanent federal income tax was created in 1913 when the Sixteenth Amendment to the Constitution was ratified. The Treasury Department collects this tax through the Internal Revenue Service (IRS). Tax returns filed each year show how much money was earned at work and how much was received from investments or other sources. The sum of all forms of income is *gross income*.

Each tax return may list a number of deductions. There is, for instance, a personal deduction for each individual listed on the form. A single person would get one deduction, and a married couple with three children would get five deductions. Other deductions include those for money invested in a retirement savings account and for donations to charities. There are deductions for home ownership expenses and the cost of moving. This part of the tax return can be hard to fill out. The figure determined by subtracting deductions from gross income is *adjusted gross income* (AGI). The adjusted gross income determines a filer's tax bracket.

There are four categories for people filing taxes, but let's look at single filers. Single filers are just what they sound like: they are not married and do not have financial responsibility for children or other dependents.

In 2004 a single filer's AGI was taxed at one of six levels, ranging from 10 percent to 35 percent. Filers with an AGI between zero and $7,150 were expected to pay 10 percent of that amount in federal income tax. A person with an AGI above $319,100 was taxed at a rate of 35 percent. What might this mean?

Suppose you have an AGI of $30,000. That places you in the 25-percent tax bracket. This means that one-quarter of your taxable income—$7,500—should be paid to the U.S. government in income tax. If most of your income came from employment, some of this tax would have been taken from each paycheck. When you fill out your income tax return, you might find that you have paid a total of $6,950 during the year. In this case, you would write a check for the difference between $7,500 and $6,950—or $550—to the Internal Revenue Service. If, however, you paid more than $7,500 in taxes during 2004, the IRS would owe you the difference.

Reading Time _____

Recalling Facts

1. The Internal Revenue Service collects taxes for
   - ❑ a. local governments.
   - ❑ b. state governments.
   - ❑ c. the federal government.

2. The sum of all forms of income listed on a tax return is called
   - ❑ a. gross income.
   - ❑ b. investment income.
   - ❑ c. adjusted gross income.

3. A deduction is allowed on tax returns for
   - ❑ a. three children.
   - ❑ b. all people living at the same address.
   - ❑ c. each person listed on the form.

4. A filer's tax bracket is decided by his or her
   - ❑ a. wealth.
   - ❑ b. adjusted gross income.
   - ❑ c. income from investments.

5. The highest tax rate for any personal income tax return filed in 2004 was
   - ❑ a. 100 percent.
   - ❑ b. 35 percent.
   - ❑ c. 25 percent.

Understanding Ideas

6. People who earn more money probably
   - ❑ a. fall into a higher tax bracket.
   - ❑ b. pay a huge amount of income tax.
   - ❑ c. avoid paying taxes.

7. It seems likely that many large families have _____ than small families.
   - ❑ a. fewer deductions
   - ❑ b. more deductions
   - ❑ c. about the same number of deductions

8. Which of the following statements is most likely to be true?
   - ❑ a. Some people who file tax returns are allowed to take deductions.
   - ❑ b. Everybody files a tax return each year.
   - ❑ c. All people who file tax returns are allowed to take at least one deduction.

9. The amount of federal income tax deducted from each paycheck is probably based on
   - ❑ a. the amount of money the job pays.
   - ❑ b. the amount of tax a person paid the previous year.
   - ❑ c. a person's adjusted gross income.

10. Which of the following is likely to have the *least* impact on a person's tax bracket?
    - ❑ a. the amount of money earned at work
    - ❑ b. the number of deductions taken
    - ❑ c. the amount of money the person saves each week

What Is Deficit Spending?

Governments create budgets once a year based on expected tax revenues (income) and expenditures (outflow). At the end of each year, if revenues have exceeded expenditures, the government has a budget surplus. Deficit spending occurs when expenditures exceed the revenues received.

At the beginning of a year, a government might expect to receive $2 million in tax revenues and spend $1.8 million during the year. That would leave a $200,000 budget surplus. Later in the year, the government might take in $100,000 less than expected in taxes and have an extra $150,000 in expenditures. The actual total tax revenues, then, are $1.9 million ($2 million − $100,000). The actual total expenditures are $1.95 million ($1.8 million + $150,000). The $1.9 million in revenues minus the $1.95 million in expenditures leaves a negative $50,000. This is deficit spending.

Deficit spending leaves a government in debt, so the government must borrow the needed money or raise extra money. The U.S. government sells bonds such as Treasury bills that give it extra money to manage its debt. If the Treasury bills offer 5 percent interest on $50,000, the government will have an additional $2,500 in expenditures the next year.

1. **Recognizing Words in Context**

   Find the word *exceeded* in the passage. One definition below is closest to the meaning of that word. One definition has the opposite or nearly the opposite meaning. The remaining definition has a completely different meaning. Label the definitions C for *closest*, O for *opposite or nearly opposite*, and D for *different*.

   _____ a. fallen short of

   _____ b. been greater than

   _____ c. passed along to

2. **Distinguishing Fact from Opinion**

   Two of the statements below present *facts*, which can be proved. The other statement is an *opinion*, which expresses someone's thoughts or beliefs. Label the statements F for *fact* and O for *opinion*.

   _____ a. When tax revenues exceed expenditures, the government has a surplus.

   _____ b. Deficit spending shows a lack of good management.

   _____ c. When expenditures exceed revenues, deficit spending occurs.

3. Keeping Events in Order

Number the statements below 1, 2, and 3 to show the order in which the events take place.

_____ a. A government subtracts expenditures from tax revenues to learn that it is deficit spending.

_____ b. A government creates a budget of expected tax revenues and expenditures.

_____ c. A government sells bonds to help support its expenditures.

4. Making Correct Inferences

Two of the statements below are correct *inferences,* or reasonable guesses. They are based on information in the passage. The other statement is an incorrect, or faulty, inference. Label the statements C for *correct* inference and F for *faulty* inference.

_____ a. When a government borrows to support its deficit, it must pay back the money it borrowed.

_____ b. When the U.S. government sells Treasury bills, the interest it pays on the bills is added to its expenditures.

_____ c. People don't mind tax raises as long as the government has a plan for spending the money.

5. Understanding Main Ideas

One of the statements below expresses the main idea of the passage. One statement is too general, or too broad. The other explains only part of the passage; it is too narrow. Label the statements M for *main idea,* B for *too broad,* and N for *too narrow.*

_____ a. Deficit spending is a means by which a government covers its expenditures.

_____ b. A government will create a budget to plan for a surplus or a deficit.

_____ c. Deficit spending leaves a government in debt.

Correct Answers, Part A _____

Correct Answers, Part B _____

Total Correct Answers _____

The Chinese numeration system is very similar to the Arabic numeration system used in the United States. The Chinese system is a base-10 system, and it uses unique characters for the numbers 0 through 9. Unlike the Arabic numeration system, where only the digits 0–9 are used in combination to form numbers greater than 9, the Chinese system also includes special characters representing 10, 100, 1,000, 10,000, and other powers of 10.

As a rule, the Chinese system expresses numbers as sums of products. For example, the number 15 in Chinese is "ten five" and means 1 ten and 5 ones. The number 30 is "three ten," or 3 tens. The number 35 is "three ten five" and actually means 3 times 10 plus 5. (In the Arabic system, we know by the relative position of the digits what each digit represents. For example, 345 means "3 hundreds, 4 tens, and 5 units," but there aren't any actual symbols for "hundreds" or "tens.")

The number 100 in Chinese is expressed with a single character, "one hundred." But the number 115 in Chinese is "one hundred one ten five," a total of four characters. Recall that the number 15 is written as just "ten five," not as "*one* ten five." The rule is that in any number larger than 99, each position must show both the amount and the place. Thus, the number 1,418 is, "one thousand four hundred one ten eight" and means 1 (number) × 1,000 (place) + 4 (number) × 100 (place) + 1 (number) × 10 (place) + eight (units).

In the Chinese system, when a zero occurs at the end of a number, it is omitted. The number 220 is "two hundred two ten" with no reference made to the zero at the end. When a single zero occurs in the middle of a number, as in the number 202, it must be expressed. The number 202 in Chinese is "two hundred zero two." When two or more zeros occur in a row, as in the number 4,007, only one zero is declared. The number 4,007 is "four thousand zero seven."

The Chinese system has its own word for "ten thousand," unlike the Arabic system, which states the number as a compound of 10 and 1,000. So the number 60,093 is "six ten-thousand zero nine ten three." This means (6 × 10,000) + (0 × 1,000) + (0 × 100) + (9 × 10) + (3).

Reading Time _____

Recalling Facts

1. The Chinese numeration system
   - ❑ a. does not use place columns.
   - ❑ b. is the same as the Arabic system.
   - ❑ c. is a base-10 system.

2. The Chinese system uses unique characters for the numbers
   - ❑ a. 1 through 5.
   - ❑ b. 1 through 9.
   - ❑ c. 0 through 9.

3. Unlike the Arabic numeration system, the Chinese system also uses special characters to represent
   - ❑ a. 1, 5, and 9.
   - ❑ b. 25, 50, and 75.
   - ❑ c. 10, 100, and 1,000.

4. The Chinese system expresses numbers as
   - ❑ a. special characters.
   - ❑ b. a base-10 system.
   - ❑ c. sums of products.

5. In the Chinese system, a zero that appears at the end of a number is
   - ❑ a. omitted.
   - ❑ b. written.
   - ❑ c. carried over to the next column.

Understanding Ideas

6. How is the number 117 written when each position must show both the amount and the place?
   - ❑ a. "one hundred one and seven"
   - ❑ b. "one hundred one ten seven"
   - ❑ c. "one hundred ten seven"

7. The number 105 in Chinese is written as
   - ❑ a. "one hundred zero five."
   - ❑ b. "one hundred five."
   - ❑ c. "one hundred zero ten five."

8. The number 4,370 in Chinese is written as
   - ❑ a. "four thousand three hundred seventy."
   - ❑ b. "four thousand three hundred seven ten."
   - ❑ c. "four thousand three hundred seven ten zero."

9. The Arabic and the Chinese numeration systems do *not* have which of the following in common?
   - ❑ a. digits 0–9 used in combination to form numbers greater than 9
   - ❑ b. base-10 system
   - ❑ c. special characters that represent 10, 100, 1,000, 10,000, and other powers of 10

10. According to the rule for when two or more zeros occur in a row, the number 55,005 is written in Chinese as
    - ❑ a. "five ten thousand five thousand zero zero five."
    - ❑ b. "five ten thousand five thousand five."
    - ❑ c. "five ten thousand five thousand zero five."

The Game of Mahjongg

Mahjongg—the Chinese game of Four Winds—emerged in the later half of the 19th century from older games. The playing pieces, called "tiles," were often beautiful works of art crafted from bamboo, bone, and ivory. During the turbulent years of the Cultural Revolution in China—the 1960s and 1970s—government officials banned the game. But mahjongg has recently regained some of its popularity.

Today the basic set contains 136 tiles. The tiles, or "cards" as they are sometimes called, come in groups. The three suits—Circle, Bamboo, and Character—are numbered one to nine; there are four tiles for each number, 108 tiles in total. There are four tiles for each of the Four Winds: North, South, East, and West. There are also four tiles for each of the Three Dragons: Red, Green, and White.

Essentially, mahjongg is a counting game. Four players representing the Four Winds arrange pairs of tiles into a square with four "walls." Each player gets a "hand" of 13 tiles from the wall; tiles are taken and discarded one at a time until someone wins. Play always moves in a counterclockwise direction. The object of the game is to collect sets of tiles: three of a kind, four of a kind, or sequences of three in the same suit. A player wins a hand—mahjongg—with four sets plus a pair.

1. **Recognizing Words in Context**

   Find the word *turbulent* in the passage. One definition below is closest to the meaning of that word. One definition has the opposite or nearly the opposite meaning. The remaining definition has a completely different meaning. Label the definitions C for *closest*, O for *opposite or nearly opposite*, and D for *different*.

   _____ a. agreeable

   _____ b. difficult

   _____ c. inferior

2. **Distinguishing Fact from Opinion**

   Two of the statements below present *facts*, which can be proved. The other statement is an *opinion*, which expresses someone's thoughts or beliefs. Label the statements F for *fact* and O for *opinion*.

   _____ a. Mahjongg tiles are beautiful works of art.

   _____ b. A mahjongg hand has 13 tiles.

   _____ c. Mahjongg players take turns playing counterclockwise around the table.

3. Keeping Events in Order

Number the statements below 1, 2, and 3 to show the order in which the events take place.

_____ a. A player calls "mahjongg."

_____ b. Pairs of tiles are arranged into a square with four "walls."

_____ c. Players take a tile and discard a tile.

4. Making Correct Inferences

Two of the statements below are correct *inferences,* or reasonable guesses. They are based on information in the passage. The other statement is an incorrect, or faulty, inference. Label the statements C for *correct* inference and F for *faulty* inference.

_____ a. Mahjongg now has the approval of the Chinese government.

_____ b. The largest number of tiles belongs to the three suits.

_____ c. It is important to remember what tiles have been played.

5. Understanding Main Ideas

One of the statements below expresses the main idea of the passage. One statement is too general, or too broad. The other explains only part of the passage; it is too narrow. Label the statements M for *main idea*, B for *too broad*, and N for *too narrow*.

_____ a. Mahjongg is a Chinese game for four players.

_____ b. Mahjongg is a Chinese game that has regained popularity since the Cultural Revolution.

_____ c. Mahjongg is a Chinese game in which players collect sets of tiles.

Correct Answers, Part A _____

Correct Answers, Part B _____

Total Correct Answers _____

On the Beat

Rhythm, meter, and syncopation are important terms in music. Rhythm refers to the movement of the music. The rhythm and the beat of a piece of music are what make the listener want to move—to twirl to a waltz or walk briskly to a march. Meter refers to the pattern of the rhythm. The meter, or pattern of stressed and unstressed beats, is expressed through units called measures.

If the meter of a piece of music is too regular, it could become monotonous or boring. Composers often add syncopation for rhythmic interest. Syncopation involves a shift in the pattern of beats. Instead of coming into a measure at the expected time, a syncopated beat will occur in an unexpected place. Some styles of music—ragtime, for instance—make extensive use of syncopation.

Rhythm and meter are expressed as fractions. Written music begins with a fraction called the time signature: ¾, ¾, and ⅝ are all common time signatures. This fraction provides two pieces of information. The numerator gives the number of beats in each measure; the denominator identifies the note that is assigned the value of one beat. The time signature ¾ shows that there are three beats in a measure, and that the quarter note will be worth one beat. Most waltzes are written in ¾ time. Many people are able to recognize the rhythm of a waltz as a pattern of three beats with the stress falling on the first beat: **one**-two-three, **one**-two-three, **one**-two-three.

The notes themselves represent fractions. A whole note resembles an empty circle; a half note is an empty circle with a straight line on either side going up or down; a quarter note is a black circle with a straight line on either side going up or down. Little "tails" on the straight line of a quarter note indicate smaller fractions. An eighth note has one tail, a sixteenth note has two tails, and so on.

The values of the notes in each measure add up to the number in the numerator of the time signature. In a typical waltz, for instance, the value of the notes in each measure must add up to three, because there are three beats per measure. For example, each measure could include three quarter notes.

The feeling expressed in a piece of music depends to a large extent on the values of the notes used. A lot of short notes, such as eighth notes, will make a waltz sound faster and more energetic. Fewer, longer notes produce a dignified, stately rhythm.

Reading Time _____

Recalling Facts

1. In music, meter refers to
   - ❏ a. the pattern of the rhythm.
   - ❏ b. the effect of syncopation.
   - ❏ c. music that twirls.

2. The time signature shows the
   - ❏ a. value of the quarter note.
   - ❏ b. number of beats in a measure.
   - ❏ c. feeling the music expresses.

3. Music is written in units called
   - ❏ a. beats.
   - ❏ b. measures.
   - ❏ c. fractions.

4. The time signature ¾ indicates that the piece is probably
   - ❏ a. a march.
   - ❏ b. in ragtime.
   - ❏ c. a waltz.

5. A shift in the beat from a stressed to an unstressed note is called
   - ❏ a. meter.
   - ❏ b. syncopation.
   - ❏ c. ragtime.

Understanding Ideas

6. Which of the following is *not* important to rhythm, meter, or syncopation?
   - ❏ a. the speed of the note
   - ❏ b. the time signature of the piece
   - ❏ c. the sound of the note

7. Which note is worth one beat in a piece with a % time signature?
   - ❏ a. a sixth note
   - ❏ b. an eighth note
   - ❏ c. a sixteenth note

8. One can infer from this passage that there is no such thing as a
   - ❏ a. thirty-second note.
   - ❏ b. forty-eighth note.
   - ❏ c. sixty-fourth note.

9. In a ¾ time signature there are _____ beats to the measure.
   - ❏ a. two
   - ❏ b. four
   - ❏ c. six

10. One can infer from this passage that studying music might help a person learn
    - ❏ a. to waltz.
    - ❏ b. art.
    - ❏ c. math.

Keep the Beat, Count Your Feet

Meter in poetry is similar to rhythm in music. Meter is determined by the particular pattern of stressed and unstressed syllables in a line of poetry. The fundamental units of meter in English poetry are the syllable, the foot, and the line.

A foot is a group of two or more syllables. There are four basic kinds of feet in English poetry, and all have different patterns of stressed and unstressed syllables. For example, an iamb and a trochee each have two syllables. An iamb has the accent on the second syllable ("hel**lo**"), and a trochee has the accent on the first syllable ("**la**ter").

The next two kinds of feet each have three syllables. An anapest has a stressed third syllable, as in "kanga**roo**," and a dactyl has a stressed first syllable, as in "**beau**ty queen."

The number of feet in each line of poetry will vary. If the meter consists of iambs or trochees, the number of syllables in each line must be divisible by two because each of these feet has two syllables. If the meter consists of anapests or dactyls, the number of syllables in each line must be divisible by three.

Here's a four-foot line by the poet Dylan Thomas that is made up of anapests: "There are **ma**/ny who **say**/that a **dog**/has his **day**."

1. **Recognizing Words in Context**

   Find the word *fundamental* in the passage. One definition below is closest to the meaning of that word. One definition has the opposite or nearly the opposite meaning. The remaining definition has a completely different meaning. Label the definitions C for *closest*, O for *opposite or nearly opposite*, and D for *different*.

   _____ a. easy

   _____ b. essential

   _____ c. secondary

2. **Distinguishing Fact from Opinion**

   Two of the statements below present *facts*, which can be proved. The other statement is an *opinion*, which expresses someone's thoughts or beliefs. Label the statements F for *fact* and O for *opinion*.

   _____ a. Counting beats takes the fun out of writing poetry.

   _____ b. A foot is group of two or more syllables.

   _____ c. An anapest has three syllables with stress on the third syllable.

3. Keeping Events in Order

Number the statements below 1, 2, and 3 to show the order in which the terms were named in the passage.

_____ a. foot

_____ b. line

_____ c. syllable

4. Making Correct Inferences

Two of the statements below are correct *inferences,* or reasonable guesses. They are based on information in the passage. The other statement is an incorrect, or faulty, inference. Label the statements C for *correct* inference and F for *faulty* inference.

_____ a. If the first line of poetry has five feet, the second line will not have five feet.

_____ b. If the meter uses a foot that has four syllables, the number of syllables in each line must be divisible by four.

_____ c. A foot with three syllables can be made up of one or more words.

5. Understanding Main Ideas

One of the statements below expresses the main idea of the passage. One statement is too general, or too broad. The other explains only part of the passage; it is too narrow. Label the statements M for *main idea*, B for *too broad*, and N for *too narrow*.

_____ a. The fundamental units of meter in English poetry are the syllable, the foot, and the line.

_____ b. There are four basic kinds of metric feet in English poetry.

_____ c. Meter is determined by the pattern of stressed and unstressed syllables.

Correct Answers, Part A _____

Correct Answers, Part B _____

Total Correct Answers _____

Fibonacci: Advancing Mathematics

Leonardo Pisano is better known by the nickname Fibonacci. He was born around 1175 in Pisa, Italy, but was educated in North Africa where his father worked. He also traveled with his father, and in his travels he learned about mathematical systems used in other countries. He recognized the advantages they had over the Roman numeral system. When Fibonacci returned to Italy around 1200, he wrote a number of books based on what he had learned. These books played an important role in reviving the study of mathematics in Europe.

Liber abaci (1202) was based on the arithmetic and algebra that Fibonacci had learned during his travels. It introduced readers to the Hindu-Arabic place-value decimal system and to the Arabic numerals that we use today. In the book, he posed the following problem: How many pairs of rabbits will be produced in a year, beginning with a single pair, if in every month each pair bears a new pair that becomes productive from the second month on?

The result is known as the Fibonacci sequence: 1, 1, 2, 3, 5, 8, 13, 21, 34, 55, . . . In this sequence, each number is the sum of the two preceding numbers. Thus 1 plus 1 is 2, 1 plus 2 is 3, 2 plus 3 is 5, and so on.

Practica geometriae (1220) contains a large collection of geometry problems. The book has useful information for surveyors, including a chapter on how to calculate the height of tall objects using similar triangles. In *Flos* (1225) Fibonacci worked out difficult problems that members of Italy's ruling class had challenged him to solve.

Liber quadratorum (1225) is a number-theory book. Fibonacci notes that all square numbers come from sums of odd numbers. As he wrote in the book: Unity is a square and from it is produced the first square, named 1. Adding 3 to this makes the second square, 4, whose root is 2. If to this sum is added a third odd number, 5, the third square will be produced, 9, whose root is 3. And so the sequence and the series of square numbers always rise through the regular addition of odd numbers.

Fibonacci was a major contributor to the foundations of modern number theory. But this theory was overlooked during the 13th century. After Fibonacci's death, his influence faded away for many centuries. Mathematics made no real progress for about another 300 years.

Reading Time _____

Recalling Facts

1. Fibonacci
   - ❑ a. was born in North Africa and traveled to Italy.
   - ❑ b. learned the mathematical systems of countries to which he traveled.
   - ❑ c. studied the Roman numeral system used in Italy.

2. *Liber abaci* was based on
   - ❑ a. arithmetic and algebra.
   - ❑ b. the Fibonacci sequence.
   - ❑ c. number theory.

3. *Practica geometriae*
   - ❑ a. contains a large collection of geometry problems.
   - ❑ b. contains solutions to problems that Fibonacci was challenged to solve.
   - ❑ c. contains a number sequence known as the Fibonacci sequence.

4. *Flos* was Fibonacci's _____ book.
   - ❑ a. fourth
   - ❑ b. second
   - ❑ c. third

5. In *Liber quadratorum,* Fibonacci notes that _____ can be constructed as sums of odd numbers.
   - ❑ a. round numbers
   - ❑ b. prime numbers
   - ❑ c. square numbers

Understanding Ideas

6. One could infer that educated people in Italy, at the end of the 12th century,
   - ❑ a. were very advanced in mathematics.
   - ❑ b. were using only simple arithmetic.
   - ❑ c. were against Fibonacci's books.

7. The book *Practica geometriae* might have sparked an interest in
   - ❑ a. writing and solving number problems.
   - ❑ b. square roots and the sequence of square numbers.
   - ❑ c. calculating the exact area of land.

8. The next number is _____ in the following Fibonacci sequence: 1, 1, 2, 3, 5, 8, 13, . . .
   - ❑ a. 18
   - ❑ b. 21
   - ❑ c. 25

9. One can infer that Fibonacci
   - ❑ a. was the most advanced mathematician of his time.
   - ❑ b. was the only mathematician during his time.
   - ❑ c. was the only person interested in mathematics during his time.

10. Which of the following statements best sums up this passage?
    - ❑ a. Fibonacci wrote a number of books that played an important role in advancing mathematics in the 13th century.
    - ❑ b. Fibonacci, a mathematician who was ahead of his time, made major contributions to math and science.
    - ❑ c. Fibonacci recognized the advantages of mathematical systems in other countries.

In mathematics, a prime number is a whole number greater than 1 whose only factors are 1 and itself. For example, the only factors of 11—or the only whole numbers you can multiply together to equal 11—are 11 and 1. Prime numbers under 25 are 2, 3, 5, 7, 11, 13, 17, 19, and 23.

Conversely, a whole number greater than 1 with factors other than 1 and itself is a composite number. Fifteen is a composite number because 3×5, like 1×15, also equals 15. So we say that the factors of 15 are 1, 3, 5, and 15.

Some factors of a composite number are prime numbers. They are called prime factors. For example, the number 12 has two prime factors. The factors of 12 are 1, 2, 3, 4, 6, and 12. The prime factors in this sequence are 2 and 3. The factors 4, 6, and 12 are not prime factors. Factors of each of these composite numbers include numbers other than 1 and itself.

Mathematicians have proved that the number of prime numbers that exist is infinite. The mathematicians use formulas based on prime factors to search for larger and larger prime numbers. Prior to computers, the largest known prime number was 44 digits long. With the aid of computer software, mathematicians have been able to find prime numbers that are more than 7,000,000 digits long!

1. **Recognizing Words in Context**

Find the words *prior to* in the passage. One definition below is closest to the meaning of that word. One definition has the opposite or nearly the opposite meaning. The remaining definition has a completely different meaning. Label the definitions C for *closest*, O for *opposite or nearly opposite*, and D for *different*.

_____ a. following

_____ b. working with

_____ c. before

2. **Distinguishing Fact from Opinion**

Two of the statements below present *facts*, which can be proved. The other statement is an *opinion*, which expresses someone's thoughts or beliefs. Label the statements F for *fact* and O for *opinion*.

_____ a. The number 11 is a prime number.

_____ b. The prime factors of 6 are 2 and 3.

_____ c. Most people do not need to know how to figure out prime numbers.

3. Keeping Events in Order

Number the statements below 1, 2, and 3 to show the order in which the events take place in the passage.

_____ a. The largest known prime number is more than 7,000,000 digits long.

_____ b. Mathematicians today use computer software to find large prime numbers.

_____ c. The largest known prime number is 44 digits long.

4. Making Correct Inferences

Two of the statements below are correct *inferences,* or reasonable guesses. They are based on information in the passage. The other statement is an incorrect, or faulty, inference. Label the statements C for *correct* inference and F for *faulty* inference.

_____ a. The number 1 is a prime number.

_____ b. The number 2 is a prime factor of any even number.

_____ c. Mathematicians rely on computers to learn more about prime numbers.

5. Understanding Main Ideas

One of the statements below expresses the main idea of the passage. One statement is too general, or too broad. The other explains only part of the passage; it is too narrow. Label the statements M for *main idea,* B for *too broad,* and N for *too narrow.*

_____ a. Mathematics is a study of numbers.

_____ b. Mathematicians have proved that the number of prime numbers is infinite.

_____ c. A prime number, unlike a composite number, has factors of only 1 and itself.

Correct Answers, Part A _____

Correct Answers, Part B _____

Total Correct Answers _____

The number zero has two important uses today. The first use is as an empty-place indicator in our place-value number system. For example, in 3,407 the zero reminds us that there is nothing in the "tens" column. The second use of zero is as an actual number. The use of zero as a number began long after the concept of zero as a place indicator had been established.

The symbol for zero as a place indicator came into use around 700 B.C.E. in Babylonia. The Babylonians had been using a place-value number system that didn't include a symbol for zero. For more than 1,000 years, until its use around 700 B.C.E., Babylonians wrote numbers such as 3,407 like this: "34 7." Later, around 400 B.C.E., the Babylonians began to use a symbol that resembles a wedge ($\wedge$) to represent the position where no digit was written. However, for the Babylonians, the wedge did not signify "the number zero" as meaning "nothing." The concept of "empty space" and "nothing" were still separate then.

While the Babylonians were using zero as a place indicator, Greek astronomers began using zero as a real number in recording their data. One explanation even suggests that the zero symbol stands for the "obol," a Greek coin that had very little value.

Many historians believe that the Indian use of zero as a number evolved from its use by Greek astronomers. The first recorded use of the number zero in India was in A.D. 876. An inscription on a stone tablet dating from that year indicates the numbers 270 and 50 almost as they appear today.

At this time, several important math rules had begun to emerge in India. One of these rules was that subtracting a number from itself results in zero ($4 - 4 = 0$). Another rule had to do with adding and subtracting positive and negative numbers. This rule showed that a positive number subtracted from zero is negative ($0 - 4 = -4$). Similarly, a negative number that is subtracted from zero is positive ($0 - -4 = 4$). A third rule stated that the product of any number multiplied by zero is zero ($4 \times 0 = 0$).

Use of the number zero began to spread west through Europe and east through China as a result of trade. It wasn't until around A.D. 1600, however, that the number zero came into worldwide use.

Reading Time _____

Recalling Facts

1. The use of zero as a number began
   _____ the concept of zero as a
   position indicator.
   - ❏ a. before
   - ❏ b. after
   - ❏ c. at the same time as

2. The first people to use a symbol to
   represent the position for zero were
   the
   - ❏ a. Babylonians.
   - ❏ b. Greeks.
   - ❏ c. Indians.

3. The first people to use zero as a real
   number were the
   - ❏ a. Babylonians.
   - ❏ b. Greeks.
   - ❏ c. Indians.

4. The first genuine recorded Indian
   use of zero occurred
   - ❏ a. in A.D. 876.
   - ❏ b. in 400 B.C.E.
   - ❏ c. in A.D. 700.

5. An inscription on a stone tablet that
   dates from A.D. 876 indicates the
   numbers
   - ❏ a. 34 and 3,407.
   - ❏ b. 27 and 750.
   - ❏ c. 270 and 50.

Understanding Ideas

6. You can conclude from the
   information in this passage that the
   - ❏ a. concept of zero as a number
     caught on quickly.
   - ❏ b. concept of zero as a number was
     difficult for the Babylonians to
     imagine.
   - ❏ c. concept of zero as a position
     indicator was never really
     understood.

7. Once the number zero came into use
   in India, mathematicians
   - ❏ a. began to use the wedge as a
     symbol for it.
   - ❏ b. started to draw it as an oval.
   - ❏ c. developed rules regarding its
     use.

8. Among the Indians' rules for zero
   are rules for
   - ❏ a. adding negative numbers.
   - ❏ b. multiplying and dividing
     numbers by zero.
   - ❏ c. adding and subtracting positive
     and negative numbers.

9. Use of the number zero began to
   spread because of
   - ❏ a. its use by Greek astronomers.
   - ❏ b. trade between India and
     European countries.
   - ❏ c. because of the use of the obol.

10. For the Babylonians,
    - ❏ a. the wedge indicated "empty
      space" and did not represent
      "nothing."
    - ❏ b. holding a place for zero was the
      same as using the number zero.
    - ❏ c. the wedge symbol meant the
      same thing as "nothing."

In the 7th century, a math scholar from India named Brahmagupta began forming rules for the use of negative numbers in arithmetic. But long before—and even after—Brahmagupta's work, negative numbers were viewed with skepticism by many. People struggled with the concept that negative numbers were less than zero, or less than nothing. Most scholars denied that negative numbers could even exist. After all, there didn't appear to be any practical reason for anyone to introduce negative numbers. One couldn't eat -2 carrots. There simply was no use for negative numbers!

Later, in cases in which negative numbers were introduced, the concept was avoided rather than embraced. Daniel Fahrenheit was one who chose to avoid the use of negative numbers when he proposed his temperature scale in 1724. By establishing the freezing point of water at 32 degrees, he showed his belief that most temperatures would appear as positive numbers.

Negative numbers finally gained a foothold in the 19th century. The concept became useful in terms of debts. If a horse cost $40 but a person paid only $25, the $15 that was owed was a debt that could be paid later.

Slowly, through the work of the mathematicians René Descartes and Leonhard Euler, negative numbers became accepted. Today negative numbers are essential elements in all branches of mathematics.

1. **Recognizing Words in Context**

   Find the word *skepticism* in the passage. One definition below is closest to the meaning of that word. One definition has the opposite or nearly the opposite meaning. The remaining definition has a completely different meaning. Label the definitions C for *closest,* O for *opposite or nearly opposite,* and D for *different.*

   _____ a. confidence

   _____ b. suspicion

   _____ c. idleness

2. **Distinguishing Fact from Opinion**

   Two of the statements below present *facts,* which can be proved. The other statement is an *opinion,* which expresses someone's thoughts or beliefs. Label the statements F for *fact* and O for *opinion.*

   _____ a. Negative numbers were in use hundreds of years before they were accepted.

   _____ b. People struggled with the concept that something can be less than nothing.

   _____ c. People should have been more accepting of the use of negative numbers.

3. Keeping Events in Order

Number the statements below 1, 2, and 3 to show the order in which the events took place.

_____ a. Fahrenheit avoided the use of negative numbers on his temperature scale.

_____ b. Rules for the use of negative numbers in arithmetic were formed in India.

_____ c. Leonhard Euler and others used negative numbers in their calculations.

4. Making Correct Inferences

Two of the statements below are correct *inferences,* or reasonable guesses. They are based on information in the passage. The other statement is an incorrect, or faulty, inference. Label the statements C for *correct* inference and F for *faulty* inference.

_____ a. Negative numbers had no practical application in many past societies.

_____ b. Brahmagupta helped bring the concept of negative numbers into everyday use in India.

_____ c. At the time Fahrenheit lived, negative numbers were not well accepted.

5. Understanding Main Ideas

One of the statements below expresses the main idea of the passage. One statement is too general, or too broad. The other explains only part of the passage; it is too narrow. Label the statements M for *main idea*, B for *too broad,* and N for *too narrow.*

_____ a. For centuries, people saw no use for negative numbers.

_____ b. The concept of negative numbers began to gain acceptance in the 19th century.

_____ c. The use of negative numbers has evolved over the last several hundred years.

Correct Answers, Part A _____

Correct Answers, Part B _____

Total Correct Answers _____

The Rise and Fall of a Dot-Com

The dot-com frenzy of the late 1990s is an investment story with a moral: Every investment in the stock market is risky. A $1,000 investment in 100 shares of stock at $10 per share might become $1,019 a week later if the share price rises to $10.19. However, in six months the stock could be trading at $9.42 per share, and the $1,000 investment would be worth only $942.

Such small changes in a stock's price are normal. Over the course of years, an investment in a well-established company would probably increase. This was not, however, the case with many of the "dot-coms"—Internet-based businesses—of the 1990s. By the late 1990s, dot-coms had become the most desirable investment around. Rumors circulated about investors doubling or tripling their money almost overnight. The truth is that too many investors gambled and lost.

Consider the case of a dot-com we'll call KickIt.com. KickIt.com earned $134,000 in 1997, but it finished the year in the red due to having about $2 million in costs. The same thing happened in 1998, and this time KickIt.com's loss was even larger. Because KickIt.com's owners needed to raise capital to keep it going, they decided to take KickIt.com public. Instead of remaining a private company, it would become a public company, and its shares would be bought and sold on the stock exchange. The money raised by selling stock would be used to pay KickIt.com's debts and, it was hoped, would also make the company profitable.

At the IPO, or initial public offering, shares in KickIt.com sold for $20. Due to high demand, the share price rose quickly. Suddenly it seemed that everyone wanted a piece of the company's success, and over the next 18 months the price exploded. When the stock price reached $118.47, many people sold their shares at a huge profit. Then the stock price began to plummet. Six months down the road, KickIt.com's stock had fallen to about $57 a share. Within a year, the company went bankrupt, and its shares were worthless.

In the end, the founders of KickIt.com made millions of dollars. A few fortunate investors also profited, but almost everyone else lost money—in some cases, millions of dollars. By the time KickIt.com collapsed, tens of billions of dollars had disappeared.

The moral of the story? The value of a company and the price of its shares do not always go hand-in-hand. The dot-com craze taught many investors an important but expensive lesson.

Reading Time _____

Recalling Facts

1. A dot-com is
   ❑ a. a Web site.
   ❑ b. a place to buy shares of stock.
   ❑ c. an Internet-based business.

2. The share price of KickIt.com reached
   ❑ a. $57.
   ❑ b. $118.47.
   ❑ c. $134,000.

3. According to this passage, any amount invested in the stock market is
   ❑ a. at risk.
   ❑ b. likely to rise over the course of years.
   ❑ c. certain to fall.

4. The owners of KickIt.com took the company public
   ❑ a. because they were greedy.
   ❑ b. in order to raise money.
   ❑ c. because private businesses are not profitable.

5. Only the _____ made millions of dollars from KickIt.com.
   ❑ a. investors
   ❑ b. stock market
   ❑ c. founders

Understanding Ideas

6. One can infer from the context that the word *plummet* means to
   ❑ a. "come down gradually."
   ❑ b. "fall very fast."
   ❑ c. "first rise, then fall."

7. Which of the following best expresses the moral to the story of KickIt.com?
   ❑ a. Don't buy a stock just because it is popular.
   ❑ b. A popular stock will make you lots of money.
   ❑ c. Dot-coms were bad investments.

8. What does it mean when a business finishes "in the red"?
   ❑ a. It earns money.
   ❑ b. It closes down.
   ❑ c. It takes a loss.

9. The top price of a share of stock in KickIt.com was about _____ its price at the IPO.
   ❑ a. three times
   ❑ b. six times
   ❑ c. ten times

10. Which of the following most likely expresses the opinion of the author?
    ❑ a. The stock market is too risky for most people.
    ❑ b. One should research a company before buying stock in it.
    ❑ c. A smart person will get rich in the stock market.

Pyramid schemes are used by phony businesses in which people invest because they are led to believe that they will make a lot of money. The promise of making money puts pressure on them to buy start-up kits of products. The investors' profits are based on the number of distributors they recruit to sell the products—not on the number of products they sell. "Investors" must pay a fee to join the pyramid, and then they get a share of the fees that are paid by the new investors they recruit. This arrangement is called a pyramid because the number of investors increases at each level.

   If you are one of the people at the top of the pyramid, you are Level 1. If you recruit six people under you, those people are Level 2, and so on. Your profit will scale up by factors of six as your distributors recruit new distributors: $6 \times 6 = 36$ for Level 3; $36 \times 6 = 216$ for Level 4; $216 \times 6 = 1,296$ for Level 5; and so on. By Level 10, the total number of people in the scheme—including yourself and all levels—will be 10,077,696. The total for Level 12 is greater than the entire U.S. population! At some point, pyramid schemes have to collapse. Investors quickly run out of potential recruits. Most distributors end up with nothing but the products they were pressured to buy.

1. Recognizing Words in Context

Find the word *recruit* in the passage. One definition below is closest to the meaning of that word. One definition has the opposite or nearly the opposite meaning. The remaining definition has a completely different meaning. Label the definitions C for *closest*, O for *opposite or nearly opposite*, and D for *different*.

_____ a. lay off

_____ b. omit

_____ c. sign up

2. Distinguishing Fact from Opinion

Two of the statements below present *facts*, which can be proved. The other statement is an *opinion*, which expresses someone's thoughts or beliefs. Label the statements F for *fact* and O for *opinion*.

_____ a. Distributors are pressured into buying start-up kits of products.

_____ b. Plans that pay money for recruiting new distributors usually collapse.

_____ c. No one loses more money than they can afford to lose in a pyramid scheme.

3. Keeping Events in Order

Number the statements below 1, 2, and 3 to show the order in which the events take place.

_____ a. The investor recruits more distributors.

_____ b. The pyramid collapses.

_____ c. The investor buys a start-up kit of products to get into the pyramid.

4. Making Correct Inferences

Two of the statements below are correct *inferences,* or reasonable guesses. They are based on information in the passage. The other statement is an incorrect, or faulty, inference. Label the statements C for *correct* inference and F for *faulty* inference.

_____ a. Pyramid schemes start out as honest businesses that sometimes lose money.

_____ b. Some businesses that seem like pyramid schemes at first are not actually pyramid schemes.

_____ c. If you get in on a pyramid scheme early, you're sure to make money.

5. Understanding Main Ideas

One of the statements below expresses the main idea of the passage. One statement is too general, or too broad. The other explains only part of the passage; it is too narrow. Label the statements M for *main idea,* B for *too broad,* and N for *too narrow.*

_____ a. In a pyramid scheme, investors are told that they will earn profits simply by recruiting more investors.

_____ b. Joining a pyramid scheme is a risky way to try to earn money.

_____ c. Pyramid schemes are used by phony businesses in which people invest because they believe they will make a lot of money.

Correct Answers, Part A _____

Correct Answers, Part B _____

Total Correct Answers _____

Using the Pythagorean Theorem

Geometry is the branch of mathematics that deals with the measurement of lines, shapes, angles, and distances. Some of the formulas used in geometry were worked out thousands of years ago when people began to draw maps and build large buildings such as pyramids. In fact, the word *geometry* comes from Greek words meaning "earth" (*geo*) and "measurement" (*metron*).

Pythagoras, a Greek mathematician who lived in the 6th century B.C.E., is credited with the discovery of a theorem about "right" or 90-degree triangles. A *theorem* is a mathematical statement that can be proved.

The Pythagorean theorem shows the relationship between the sides of a right triangle. A right triangle always includes one 90-degree angle. If lines a and b are the sides of the triangle that form a right angle, and c is the hypotenuse—or the side opposite the right angle—then $a^2 + b^2 = c^2$. The exponent 2 indicates that the number must be squared; that is, multiplied by itself. Consider a right triangle where a equals 6 and b equals 8. Six squared (or 6 times 6) equals 36, and 8 squared equals 64. Add a (36) and b (64) to get c squared, or 100. To find c you must find the square root of 100, which is 10.

The Pythagorean theorem is a very useful bit of mathematics. For instance, it provides a way to determine whether an angle measures exactly 90 degrees. This is handy if you need to know whether the bookcase you have just assembled has "square" or 90-degree corners.

The Pythagorean theorem is also a system for calculating distance. As the catcher on a baseball team, I have to throw the ball from home plate to second base. How far is that? I know that the bases on the diamond are 90 feet apart. The line from home plate to second base is the hypotenuse of a right triangle formed by home plate, first base, and second base. I set up the question in the form of the Pythagorean theorem. Ninety feet squared is 8,100, and 8,100 feet plus 8,100 feet equals 16,200 feet. It is difficult to figure out the square root of this number, but I use my calculator and discover that the square root of 16,200 is a number between 127 and 128. It is obvious to me that I need to practice throwing the ball until I can throw it farther than 127 feet.

Reading Time _____

Recalling Facts

1. Geometry can be used to
   - ❑ a. prove a theorem.
   - ❑ b. multiply numbers.
   - ❑ c. measure shapes.

2. The Pythagorean theorem as stated in the passage is
   - ❑ a. *a* squared times *b* squared equals *c* squared.
   - ❑ b. *a* squared plus *b* squared equals *c* squared.
   - ❑ c. *a* squared plus *b* squared equals *c*.

3. To "square" a number means to
   - ❑ a. multiply it by itself.
   - ❑ b. add it to itself.
   - ❑ c. divide it by itself.

4. A 90-degree angle can also be called a
   - ❑ a. left angle.
   - ❑ b. rectangle.
   - ❑ c. right angle.

5. A right triangle has
   - ❑ a. three right angles.
   - ❑ b. two right angles.
   - ❑ c. one right angle.

Understanding Ideas

6. According to the Pythagorean theorem, if side *a* of a right triangle is 3 inches and side *b* is 4 inches, the hypotenuse must be
   - ❑ a. 5 inches.
   - ❑ b. 10 inches.
   - ❑ c. 25 inches.

7. In a three-sided figure, if $a^2 + b^2$ does *not* equal c^2, then the figure is
   - ❑ a. not a triangle.
   - ❑ b. not a right triangle.
   - ❑ c. a pyramid.

8. The Pythagorean theorem provides a way to
   - ❑ a. measure all three angles of a triangle.
   - ❑ b. calculate the size of a right angle.
   - ❑ c. use two sides of a right triangle to find the length of the third side.

9. A baseball diamond is actually a
   - ❑ a. rectangle.
   - ❑ b. square.
   - ❑ c. right triangle.

10. To use the Pythagorean theorem, one has to
   - ❑ a. know the square roots of all numbers.
   - ❑ b. own a calculator.
   - ❑ c. have a way to find the square root of any number.

Theano and the Golden Mean

Before Theano became the wife of the 6th-century Greek mathematician Pythagoras, she had been his pupil. Theano taught mathematics at Pythagoras's schools, and with the help of their three daughters, she ran the schools after his death. Theano was respected for her work in mathematics and astronomy, and her books were widely studied. One of Theano's most influential books explored the idea of the Golden Mean. The Golden Mean is also called the Golden Ratio.

First noticed as a pleasing proportion that is common in nature, the Golden Mean is the mathematical relationship, or ratio, between two measurements. Think about a line (ABC) that is divided into two unequal parts. In the Golden Mean, the ratio of the longer part (AB) to the shorter part (BC) will be the same as the ratio of the whole line (ABC) to the longer part (AB). The value of this ratio will be approximately 1.618.

The Golden Mean is manifest in the human face and body as well as in the spiral form of a seashell. Many artists compose their paintings according to the Golden Mean. Architects design buildings using the Golden Rectangle. The measurements of each part of the building—the rooms, windows, and doors—are based on the measurements of the whole. The measurements of each element also can be expressed in terms of the Golden Mean.

1. Recognizing Words in Context

Find the word *manifest* in the passage. One definition below is closest to the meaning of that word. One definition has the opposite or nearly the opposite meaning. The remaining definition has a completely different meaning. Label the definitions C for *closest*, O for *opposite or nearly opposite*, and D for *different*.

_____ a. visible

_____ b. absent

_____ c. traditional

2. Distinguishing Fact from Opinion

Two of the statements below present *facts*, which can be proved. The other statement is an *opinion*, which expresses someone's thoughts or beliefs. Label the statements F for *fact* and O for *opinion*.

_____ a. Good paintings are created according to the Golden Mean.

_____ b. One of Theano's books explored the idea of the Golden Mean.

_____ c. The Golden Mean appears in the forms of some seashells.

3. Keeping Events in Order

Number the statements below 1, 2, and 3 to show the order in which the events took place.

_____ a. Architects began to use the Golden Mean to design buildings.

_____ b. Mathematicians identified a ratio now called the Golden Mean.

_____ c. People noticed a pleasing proportion common in nature.

4. Making Correct Inferences

Two of the statements below are correct *inferences*, or reasonable guesses. They are based on information in the passage. The other statement is an incorrect, or faulty, inference. Label the statements C for *correct* inference and F for *faulty* inference.

_____ a. Women were as well-educated as men in 6th-century Greece.

_____ b. In a room based on the Golden Mean, the ratio of the door's height to its width would be 1.618.

_____ c. The Golden Rectangle expresses the same idea as the Golden Mean.

5. Understanding Main Ideas

One of the statements below expresses the main idea of the passage. One statement is too general, or too broad. The other explains only part of the passage; it is too narrow. Label the statements M for *main idea*, B for *too broad*, and N for *too narrow*.

_____ a. The Greek mathematician Theano explained the idea of the Golden Mean.

_____ b. The Greeks made many discoveries in mathematics.

_____ c. The value of the ratio called the Golden Mean is 1.618.

Correct Answers, Part A _____

Correct Answers, Part B _____

Total Correct Answers _____

ANSWER KEY

READING RATE GRAPH

COMPREHENSION SCORE GRAPH

COMPREHENSION SKILLS PROFILE GRAPH

ANSWER KEY

1A	1. a	2. a	3. b	4. c	5. a	6. a	7. c	8. b	9. a	10. a
1B	1. C, O, D	2. O, F, F	3. 1, 2, 3	4. F, C, C	5. B, N, M					
2A	1. b	2. a	3. b	4. c	5. a	6. b	7. a	8. c	9. b	10. b
2B	1. O, C, D	2. F, F, O	3. S, B, S	4. C, F, C	5. N, M, B					
3A	1. b	2. a	3. c	4. b	5. a	6. a	7. c	8. b	9. b	10. c
3B	1. O, D, C	2. O, F, F	3. 2, 3, 1	4. F, C, C	5. M, N, B					
4A	1. a	2. b	3. c	4. a	5. a	6. c	7. a	8. a	9. c	10. a
4B	1. C, O, D	2. F, F, O	3. 2, 1, 3	4. C, C, F	5. B, M, N					
5A	1. c	2. a	3. c	4. b	5. a	6. c	7. b	8. a	9. a	10. b
5B	1. O, D, C	2. F, O, F	3. 2, 3, 1	4. F, C, C	5. N, M, B					
6A	1. b	2. a	3. b	4. a	5. c	6. a	7. c	8. b	9. b	10. b
6B	1. O, D, C	2. O, F, F	3. 3, 2, 1	4. C, C, F	5. M, N, B					
7A	1. c	2. c	3. a	4. b	5. b	6. c	7. c	8. a	9. a	10. b
7B	1. C, D, O	2. F, F, O	3. 1, 2, 3	4. C, C, F	5. N, B, M					
8A	1. c	2. c	3. a	4. a	5. b	6. b	7. a	8. c	9. b	10. a
8B	1. O, C, D	2. F, O, F	3. 3, 2, 1	4. C, F, C	5. B, N, M					

9A	1. c	2. a	3. c	4. b	5. b	6. a	7. b	8. c	9. a	10. c
9B	1. O, C, D	2. F, O, F	3. 2, 1, 3	4. C, C, F	5. M, B, N					
10A	1. c	2. c	3. c	4. c	5. a	6. b	7. a	8. b	9. c	10. c
10B	1. O, C, D	2. O, F, F	3. 3, 1, 2	4. F, C, C	5. B, N, M					
11A	1. a	2. b	3. b	4. c	5. b	6. c	7. b	8. b	9. a	10. c
11B	1. D, C, O	2. O, F, F	3. 2, 3, 1	4. F, C, C	5. M, N, B					
12A	1. b	2. a	3. a	4. c	5. c	6. b	7. c	8. b	9. a	10. b
12B	1. O, D, C	2. F, F, O	3. 3, 2, 1	4. F, C, C	5. B, N, M					
13A	1. b	2. a	3. b	4. a	5. c	6. b	7. c	8. c	9. b	10. a
13B	1. O, C, D	2. F, F, O	3. 2, 1, 3	4. C, F, C	5. B, N, M					
14A	1. c	2. b	3. a	4. b	5. c	6. b	7. a	8. c	9. b	10. b
14B	1. O, D, C	2. F, F, O	3. 2, 3, 1	4. F, C, C	5. N, B, M					
15A	1. c	2. b	3. a	4. c	5. c	6. a	7. b	8. c	9. b	10. c
15B	1. C, O, D	2. O, F, F	3. 3, 2, 1	4. F, C, C	5. M, B, N					

READING RATE

Put an X on the line above each lesson number to show your reading time and words-per-minute rate for that lesson.

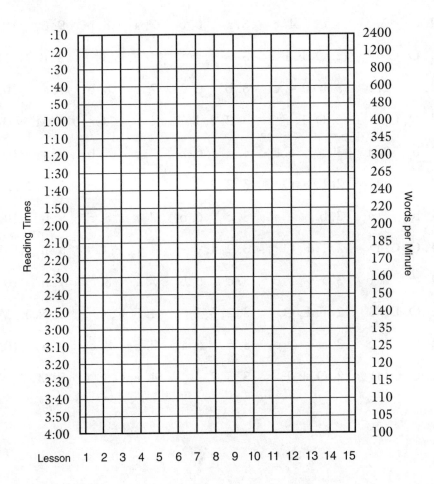

COMPREHENSION SCORE

Put an X on the line above each lesson number to indicate your total correct answers and comprehension score for that lesson.

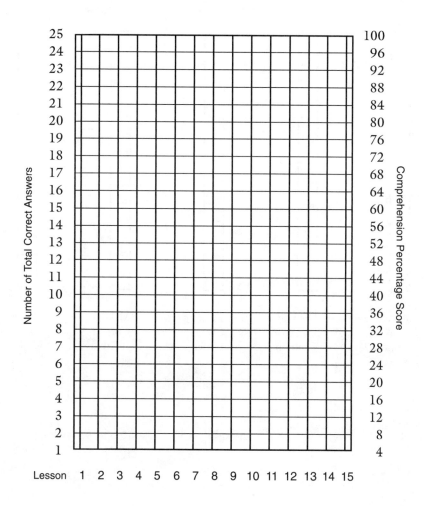

COMPREHENSION SKILLS PROFILE

Put an X in the box above each question type to indicate an incorrect response to any part of that question.

Lesson	Recognizing Words in Context	Distinguishing Fact from Opinion	Keeping Events in Order	Making Correct Inferences	Understanding Main Ideas
1					
2					
3					
4					
5					
6					
7					
8					
9					
10					
11					
12					
13					
14					
15					